STORM ORPHAN

A MEMOIR

Marsha Barrett

◆ FriesenPress

Suite 300 - 990 Fort St
Victoria, BC, V8V 3K2
Canada

www.friesenpress.com

Copyright © 2021 by Marsha Barrett
First Edition — 2021

Excerpt(s) from WE HAVE ALWAYS BEEN HERE: A QUEER MUSLIM MEMOIR by Samra Habib
Copyright © 2019 Samra Habib. Reprinted by permission of Viking Canada, a division of Penguin Random House Canada Limited. All rights reserved.

Cover image - Ron Ridley

Back cover author photo - Sarah O'Neill Springthorpe

All rights reserved.

No part of this publication may be reproduced in any form, or by any means, electronic or mechanical, including photocopying, recording, or any information browsing, storage, or retrieval system, without permission in writing from FriesenPress.

ISBN
978-1-5255-9761-9 (Hardcover)
978-1-5255-9760-2 (Paperback)
978-1-5255-9762-6 (eBook)

1. Biography & Autobiography, Personal Memoirs

Distributed to the trade by The Ingram Book Company

Authors Note

All events are true but this is a work of memory and perception. Inclusion and/or exclusion of individuals was based purely on decisions that would enhance clarity and storyline. Some names have been changed to maintain confidentiality.

For Sarah and Garrett

"A person's childhood home is the prologue to their story."

Samra Habib

Table of Contents

CHAPTER 1:	*Storm Orphan*	1
CHAPTER 2:	*Death*	5
CHAPTER 3:	*The Milkman's Daughter*	9
CHAPTER 4:	*Moon Glow*	13
CHAPTER 5:	*A Mother's Love*	17
CHAPTER 6:	*Mother's Helpers – Daddy's Dalliances*	21
CHAPTER 7:	*Button Nose*	25
CHAPTER 8:	*Grief*	29
CHAPTER 9:	*Domestic Dilemmas*	33
CHAPTER 10:	*Camp Oconto*	39
CHAPTER 11:	*The Strains*	45
CHAPTER 12:	*B61*	49
CHAPTER 13:	*Carol*	53
CHAPTER 14:	*A Stepmother*	57
CHAPTER 15:	*The Den*	61
CHAPTER 16:	*Rituals*	65
CHAPTER 17:	*Another Death*	69
CHAPTER 18:	*The Gruesome Threesome*	73
CHAPTER 19:	*Getting around Hoggs Hollow*	77
CHAPTER 20:	*Friends in the Valley*	81
CHAPTER 21:	*Henry*	87

CHAPTER 22: *"Kennel Up"*		91
CHAPTER 23: *Mrs. Williams*		95
CHAPTER 24: *Piano Lessons*		99
CHAPTER 25: *Blossoming Sexuality*		103
CHAPTER 26: *Wedding Bells*		107
CHAPTER 27: *Punishment and Padlocks*		111
CHAPTER 28: *Wherever You Walk*		117
CHAPTER 29: *New Horizons*		121
CHAPTER 30: *A Kindred Spirit*		127
CHAPTER 31: *Hash Hijinks*		131
CHAPTER 32: *Fault Line*		135
CHAPTER 33: *Déjà Vu*		139
CHAPTER 34: *To Ski or Not to Ski*		143
CHAPTER 35: *Love and Rage*		147
CHAPTER 36: *Summer Sanctuaries*		151
CHAPTER 37: *Bay Boys*		157
CHAPTER 38: *Hippie High*		161
CHAPTER 39: *Tomcats*		165
CHAPTER 40: *Working World*		171
CHAPTER 41: *Love, Dreams, and Delusions*		173
CHAPTER 42: *Shock and Awe*		179
CHAPTER 43: *Taking Flight*		183
CHAPTER 44: *Grounded*		189

CHAPTER 45: *Escape*	195
CHAPTER 46: *Down and Out*	199
CHAPTER 47: *Sunny View*	203
CHAPTER 48: *Piano Crescendo*	207
CHAPTER 49: *Reunion*	211
CHAPTER 50: *A Real Apartment*	215
CHAPTER 51: *Calamity Gary*	219
CHAPTER 52: *A Change of Direction*	223
CHAPTER 53: *Homecoming*	225
CHAPTER 54: *An Unsettling Goodbye*	231
CHAPTER 55: *New Neighbours*	233
CHAPTER 56: *Fireworks*	235
CHAPTER 57: *Life and Death*	241
CHAPTER 58: *A Brother*	245
CHAPTER 59: *Robbed*	249
CHAPTER 60: *Florida Escape*	253
CHAPTER 61: *California*	255
CHAPTER 62: *Homeless*	259
CHAPTER 63: *Greece*	261
CHAPTER 64: *Home*	269
EPILOGUE	273
ACKNOWLEDGEMENTS	277

Chapter 1
Storm Orphan

"77 PLYMBRIDGE" IS MY PASSWORD FOR ALL THOSE INTERNET accounts you have to create to purchase tickets, books, or register for bill payments. It's an address embedded in my memory, like the words to a catchy commercial jingle from the past. Now you know my password and can perhaps find a way to access all my personal information. It doesn't matter. I'm going to reveal all about myself anyway, so there will be little left to hack after this story is told.

77 Plymbridge is the address of the family home where I was born, raised, and given my name, Marsha Ellen Barrett. I lived there for almost two decades (minus a few tumultuous teenage years). A two-storey Cape Cod–style white house with real wood siding, black shutters, and a white picket fence, it was, on the outside, the image of a perfect middle-class suburban home. On the inside, life was not so perfect. The interior held rooms and hallways full of secrets, suicide, illness, and death.

Joy and laughter did exist, but as my father said once while we ate at The Steak Pit for our monthly barbecued rib dinner: "The happy times in life are like bursts of sunshine on mostly cloudy days."

As I dipped my succulent rib into the sauce (we always ordered dipping sauce on the side), I recall disagreeing with my father.

"I think it's the opposite, Daddy. Life is full of sunshine, with some cloudy days in between."

He sucked his teeth, removing the last bits of pork that remained lodged there, sighed, and wiped his thin mouth with the moist towelettes that came at the end of every meal. "You're only twelve. Wait until you're older and you'll see life differently."

I didn't respond at the time. The only sound I made was the gnawing of the last of my back ribs. It was a pleasurable goal of mine – still is – to remove every morsel of meat, gristle, or fat whenever I eat anything with a bone. Actually, it's a family trait; my father and two older sisters, Connie and Wendy, clean bones this way as well. This became an excellent way of assessing any potential partners that my sisters were dating. We served chicken and then judged how well their dates cleaned their bones at dinner. Suitors who left chicken bones with enough fleshy meat to serve a family of four were quickly rejected.

Bone-cleaning similarities aside, when my father shared his pessimistic view of life, I didn't agree with his philosophy. As a sixty-three-year-old adult, now eight years older than my father lived to be, I still don't agree.

Our family home was built in the 1950s by my father and was located in what was known as Hoggs Hollow, or "the valley," in a suburb by York Mills and Yonge Street in Toronto. My friends Leigh, Valerie, Susan, and I were valley girls long before it was coined as a name for wealthy teenagers in California. Nestled in a neighbourhood with mature trees and the meandering Don River in our backyard, the valley was a lush green setting far from the main streets, creating a rural oasis in the midst of North Toronto.

My father, Gilbert (his friends called him Gil), didn't physically build the house himself, but he purchased the land and had our home professionally designed and constructed, so it was one of a kind. All the houses in the valley were created this way. There was no mass suburban plan for the valley so each unique home was constructed over time. Our house was built in the early days of the developing neighbourhood, and there was controversy over whether we could actually live there. No Jews allowed. My father had to fight the anti-Semitism that existed everywhere at that time. I suppose the Valley Neighbourhood Association had a vision of creating a WASP community, but my father, an olive-skinned Jewish man, challenged that idea. Daddy was short, but his power and chutzpah belied his five-foot-six frame. He fought the Valley Neighbourhood Association, bulldozing his way into the wealthy white Christian enclave.

My life at 77 Plymbridge had many cloudy days and some stormy ones too. I understood my father's perception that life was challenging.

I was six when my mother died of cervical cancer. It was a devastating loss that coloured every part of my world like black crayon scratch art. My mother, Elizabeth (called Betty by her friends), was diagnosed with cancer after I was born in 1957. It was her second bout with the disease. She had been in remission for five years until my birth. As a result, my birth and her death are etched in my mind as cause and effect. While rationally I know that I didn't cause her death, the circumstances and timing of my birth were a contributing factor in how both Connie and Wendy saw their lives before I was born when "Mommy was healthy" and after I was born and she became sick.

"Everything was perfect in our family before you were born," Connie said wistfully one day when we were reminiscing as adults about our early family life.

Even though I was in my fifties by then, this comment she made so casually hurt me to my core. I know Connie's intent wasn't to hurt and she was likely thinking of her own pain at losing a mother when she was only fifteen years old.

My birth also came three years after Hurricane Hazel, the most famous storm in Canadian history, struck Southern Ontario. Although I was too young to have memories of Hazel myself, I do remember hearing adults reminisce about the hurricane and the devastation that affected so many lives and communities. One story about little Nancy Thorpe struck a chord with me.

Nancy was a four-month-old baby who was the only survivor of a family from Island Road in Long Branch and was dubbed the "storm orphan." As the hurricane wreaked havoc everywhere, a fire chief managed to get to the Thorpes' home and retrieve Nancy from her mother's arms. He carried the infant across the road to safety and then went back to assist the rest of the family. But when he returned, he discovered that the house had floated away.

I view myself as a storm orphan who has lived through a hurricane of family loss and pain. My house at 77 Plymbridge didn't float away, but my family did.

Chapter 2
Death

THE YEAR 1964 WAS ONE OF IMPENDING CHANGE. THE BEATLES' *Second Album* was released in the United States and for the first time the U.S. Surgeon General reported that smoking may be hazardous to your health. Martin Luther King was on the cover of *Time Magazine* as "Man of the Year." All the significant and newsworthy events in Toronto centred around American news. I remember seeing images on television of Lyndon B. Johnson's big right hand placed on a bible as he was sworn in as president of the United States in 1963 after John F. Kennedy's assassination.

In my world, January 1964 meant the death of Mommy – my sisters and I always called our parents Mommy and Daddy, never graduating to the more formal monikers of Mom and Dad. She died two months after Kennedy was shot. For many years I put the death of JFK and Mommy together, believing that these two catastrophes had happened at the same time. With these events happening only two months apart, it's clear to see how a six-year-old child could easily connect these two deaths. The world grieved JFK's death and I watched the images repeat on our big wood-encased television with Connie, Wendy, and Daddy. First there was the footage of the president being shot in his long black limousine with his wife, Jackie, by his side in her soft pink suit and matching pillbox hat. The televised state funeral showed thousands of people lining the street to watch the coffin go by. It seemed odd that such a large crowd was eerily silent. The only movement was people's heads slowly rotating as they followed the hearse inching down the empty street. Jackie stood with her children, Caroline and John, the pink hat now replaced by a black one with a sheer netted veil covering her face. Her children were stoic in their grief. Little John, not more than three years old, saluted the casket as it went by and Caroline, who was my age, didn't shed a tear, standing up stiff and straight by her mother's side.

My father's message to me after Mommy died was "Be strong, like the Kennedy children." I figured their grief was much larger than mine, so if they could carry on without showing tears and sadness, surely I could summon up the courage to do the same.

Following the cancer diagnosis after my birth, my mother's decline was gradual. She went through cobalt-60 radiation treatment several times over five years, which was the regimen for treating cancer in the 1950s and 1960s. I don't remember this. I only knew my mother was fine and then she was sick. No one told me anything.

I recall only one visit to the Toronto General Hospital, where my mother stayed for several months, but likely there were more. As I was lifted up to kiss her, a pungent odour enveloped me. It was a smell I'd never encountered before, like bad breath as a result of unbrushed teeth mixed with the scent of rotting garbage. I recoiled at the stench, yet was drawn to the need for affection from my mother, so I experienced a confusing mixture of desire and disgust.

At her request, no friends or relatives were allowed to visit her at the hospital. How she looked to others mattered to her. You never saw her dishevelled, half-dressed, or without makeup. Even my mother's best friend, Elenor Schacter, whom she talked to daily – sometimes three or four times a day before she went into the hospital – was discouraged from visiting.

"You know," Elenor told my sisters and me several years after Mommy's death, "I drove to the hospital every day and looked up at that building where Betty lay dying and wanted more than anything to go inside and visit her, but your father absolutely discouraged this."

Elenor lifted up her cat-eye glasses, keeping the earpieces in place, while her left hand dabbed under both eyes carefully with a balled-up tissue to stop her tear-soaked black mascara from running down her cheek.

"Once your father gives an order, it's followed. Your father," Elenor said, "is a man who is hardened around the edges and has a temper that can erupt like Mount Vesuvius, but he was devoted and loving to Betty at the end. He built a wall around her in that hospital bed that no one could break down."

One evening my father came home after a hospital visit and said he had a present for me from Mommy. Thrilled upon hearing the word *present*, I bounded into the kitchen to receive my gift. The fact that it was from my mother was significant and I didn't question the logistics of how she could possibly purchase a gift for me while lying in her hospital bed. I tore open the thin, crackling brown paper bag, overlooking the cash register receipt from the Toronto General Hospital gift shop that slipped to the floor, and clutched a twelve-inch stuffed animal. It was a grey-coloured kangaroo with a small white pouch in its front that opened to make room for a baby. There was no baby that came with it and it wasn't a soft cuddly animal. The stuffing was hard and crunchy when you squished it, like straw, but no matter, I loved the little animal and it meant Mommy was thinking of me. I treasured this mamma kangaroo and hugged it close to me.

"Is Mommy going to die?" I asked my father, as it appeared the mood in the house had shifted to one of silence and sadness and my father was spending more and more time at the hospital. He looked directly at me but didn't respond. I had that feeling that I was in trouble, but there was something else in my dad's look that I couldn't quite understand. I didn't get an answer and I knew not to ask that question again.

Several days after receiving my kangaroo, it disappeared. I carried it with me always, so I didn't see how it could get lost. Crying and despondent, I asked Wendy, "Have you seen my kangaroo? The little grey one that Mommy gave me?" My sister shook her head. Her pursed lips and lack of eye contact indicated that she either didn't care or hadn't seen it. I felt a sudden sense of urgency and fear that if I lost this gift from my mother, something bad would happen.

At that moment my father called to me from downstairs. "Marsha, we have to go to the hospital. Come get ready."

"I can't find my kangaroo, I don't want to go," I sobbed as I descended the stairs to my father's voice bellowing in the front hallway.

"We don't have time to go looking for that right now, we'll find it later," my father said tensely.

"No, I *have* to have it!" I wailed as he ignored my pleas and impatiently stuffed my arms into my too-tight winter coat.

I cried when he took me outside into the cold air, where I waited with Connie and Wendy on the snow-covered driveway while he slowly backed the big green car out of the garage to take us to the hospital. I begrudgingly climbed into the car and my father got out to close the large white garage door with its silver handle. Just before closing the door, he stooped down and picked something off the grey cement garage floor. I couldn't see what it was, but when my father got back into the car, he had a half smile on his face. He turned to me in the back seat and said, "Guess what? I found your kangaroo."

By this point, my crying had somewhat subsided and I was breathing in and out in those jerky breaths one has after intense crying. I felt pure and utter joy at this discovery. All would be right with the world! As my father passed the kangaroo over to me in the back seat, my heart sank. The kangaroo's straw stuffing was coming out, the fabric was ripped, a black button eye was missing, and its body was no longer round but flattened.

"It must have fallen out of the car and I ran over it by accident," said my father in a half-hearted apology.

At that moment I suddenly knew the response to my earlier unanswered question. My mother was going to die.

Chapter 3
The Milkman's Daughter

THE CIRCUMSTANCES OF MY BIRTH SOUNDED SUSPECT BECAUSE I was often referred to as "the milkman's daughter." In the late 1950s and early 1960s, milk was delivered to our door by an elderly gentleman named Rudy, who drove a white courier van with doors that were always open. Rudy was white and not just his skin colour. He wore white pants, a white shirt, and a white police-officer-style hat with a white plastic brim. The milk came in beautifully shaped glass bottles with thin cardboard lids that lifted with a small flap. I always found it exciting to open the front door in the morning and find two quart-sized bottles of milk waiting there.

My friend Glorianne Naiman, who lived down the street, had a little wooden trap door that opened on both the outside *and* inside of the house and her family's milk was deposited there. When I found this door at Glorianne's, I was envious, not just about the child-sized white door with the wooden knob but for the treasures it held. Who knew that the milkman also delivered ice cream and bread? My parents kept this a secret from me, I guess, so I wouldn't demand any treats.

As a young child, my lineage as the milkman's daughter seemed mysterious and perplexing. I didn't know this was a phrase coined at the time to signify someone who looked different from the rest of their family. My mother, father, and two older sisters all had dark hair and brown eyes, affirming their Jewish heritage. I, on the other hand, had blue eyes and curly blond hair. "Spun gold," my father often called me, referring to my golden locks. I loved it when he called me this because it conjured up images of fairy tales and princesses, much more enchanting and legitimate than the milkman's daughter.

My sisters Connie and Wendy were aged nine and six respectively when I was born, so it had appeared that my parents' days of having babies were done. My mother was surprised to find herself pregnant with me at age thirty-six, and I often heard that my birth was unplanned. You can see how this information, along with my golden hair, had me suspiciously eyeing Rudy each week, wondering if he'd ever delivered more than milk.

Our house on 77 Plymbridge had not been designed for three children as there were only three bedrooms: two upstairs and my parents' bedroom on the main floor. A space for my crib was created by removing a desk from a small alcove upstairs that had a sloping ceiling on one side and a shelf of books on the opposite straight wall. My first memory is of climbing out of that crib and sitting in the alcove surrounded by books, perhaps an early introduction that led to my love of reading.

At the time of my birth, my mother was an attractive thirty-six-year-old woman. She had deep-set brown eyes and black hair freshly combed back from her receding hairline and worn in a short bob, the style of the day. She had a calm and serious demeanour, and no matter what she was doing, she appeared well-groomed. People described her as a "lady who carried herself well." She dressed stylishly in twin cashmere sweater sets and wool skirts often paired with a string of cultured pearls and matching pearl stud earrings that my father had purchased on one of his business trips to Japan.

My father, only a few years older than my mother, had wavy black hair, a slim build, and skin colour that could pass for a number of different ethnicities: Italian, Spanish, or Middle Eastern. He enhanced his olive skin by tanning, often in the nude in our backyard, to ensure no tan lines. He was physically fit and took care of his health by watching what he ate and drank. His only vice was smoking. He enjoyed cigars and had a collection of pipes that he displayed in our family room, which we called the den. I learned about meerschaum pipes at an early age. I was fascinated with the intricately carved pipes that looked like ivory and turned to incremental shades of yellow and amber after Daddy had smoked them for a while.

Daddy was a successful businessman, a chartered accountant who started his own company. He was ambitious, driven, and really only had two moods: the first was fun and playful with a good sense of humour, the life of the party.

On our regular weekend ski days at Collingwood, he would yell, "Hey, boobies, bend your knees!" at the top of his lungs as he rode the chairlift up and saw Connie, Wendy, and me traversing down the hill. While I was mortified that he used this word, he called out in such a humorous way that even though I was embarrassed, it also made me smile on the inside. I felt noticed and loved.

His other mood was angry, irritable, impatient, and demanding. Getting ready to go skiing was often tense, as we packed the car with all the required equipment in the limited time we had, in order to be first on the hill when the lifts opened. "Lifts open at 8:30 and the first run is the best of the day," he barked while we all scrambled bleary-eyed at the crack of dawn to meet this required deadline.

It was true. Setting the first tracks down on a blanket of fresh snow was both exhilarating and peaceful. It felt like we were alone in the world as we forged a path through the powder, the only sound the steady rhythm of our skis carving their way through the snow.

Thanks to Daddy, I learned to ski at an early age and loved the thrill of the hill. He taught me to sing when you go down the hill and to look out at the view, not down at your skis. We drank red wine from a leather wineskin that he slung across him like a woman's shoulder bag. Daddy ascribed to the European philosophy of wine drinking as a natural beverage. He thought kids would be less enamoured of alcohol if it was consumed in small amounts together as a family. At the end of a day of skiing, he always said, no matter what, "What a perfect day!" If for some reason I missed a ski day, he'd say to me when he came home, "You missed a perfect day, Marsha!"

Together my parents made a striking couple. In all the family photos, they look like movie stars, with their fashionable clothes, sunglasses, and healthy glow set against a backdrop of fancy cars and vacation vistas: golfing trips to Florida, skiing in the Alps, cruising on our thirty-two-foot yacht, which was kept at Lake Simcoe.

I was raised as a princess, not a milkman's daughter.

Chapter 4
Moon Glow

JEWS AND CHINESE FOOD GO TOGETHER LIKE SOAP ON A ROPE. CAN you still buy this? It was a great invention, as soap gets slimy sitting in that shower dish. Adding a rope avoided that. There was a theory that soap on a rope was invented by prisons, so it couldn't be dropped. On special occasions, such as Father's Day or Chanukah, I always bought my father one of these soaps attached to a soft, thick braided white rope: either the round South Sea–scented Old Spice soap or the rectangular-shaped English Leather one, which had a musky cedar scent, nothing like leather.

On Christmas Day you can count on finding Chinese restaurants and movie theatres filled with Jews. In the 1960s there used to be no other restaurants open on Christmas. During the time I grew up, both groups were considered outsiders, not part of the mainstream. Perhaps the Jewish affinity for Chinese food reveals our common bond of being foreigners, both groups often held in rein with invisible ropes around our necks.

There were only two restaurants where we ate so-called Chinese food, ordered from a Cantonese-Canadian menu. If we were going out to eat, then we went to Moonglow on Yonge Street. For takeout, we consistently ordered from Sea-Hi on Bathurst Street, always on a Sunday night, while watching Walt Disney's show on television. These two restaurants were clients of my father's. As a chartered accountant with his own firm, he looked after their books and said it was important to give them the business. But we all knew we really only ate at these two restaurants because my father got a discount.

We also always ordered the same food: breaded chicken balls with luminous red sweet and sour sauce (nothing sour about it), pork fried rice, and barbecued pork ribs. We obviously weren't *those* kind of Jews, who kept kosher.

Inside Moonglow, there was a small red carpeted bridge you crossed over. The pool of water underneath was filled with gigantic goldfish whose mouths opened wide like baby birds waiting for their mother to feed them. I was mesmerized by these fish and often had to be dragged away from the bridge to sit at the table and eat my dinner. The end of the meal was my next favourite part of visiting Moonglow. Waiters dressed in black suits with freshly pressed white shirts came to our table and, using silver tongs, presented each of us with a steaming-hot, damp white terrycloth to wipe our mouths and hands. The warmth of the cloth against my face as I wiped the remaining residue of sticky red sweet and sour sauce off my lips was heavenly. Then, the highlight of the evening, fortune cookies – one for each person – were placed in the middle of the table and you were to take the one that pointed to you. These hard almond-coloured cookies that folded in on themselves held excitement and possibility. I didn't care about eating the dry, tasteless cookies; only the fortune inside held my interest.

One evening at Moonglow, I chose the fortune cookie that was closest to me and cracked it open with two hands. There was little worry about germs and bacteria back then, so there were no plastic wrappers to detract from the visceral experience of immediately crumbling the cookie's hard and somewhat shiny exterior. I retrieved the slip of white paper that held important information about my future. Too young to read, I passed it to my father.

"What does it say? What does it say?" I asked impatiently, as only a five-year-old would.

"'An unexpected event will soon be approaching. You must be patient,'" my father read in a slow and steady voice.

"What does that mean, Daddy?" I asked.

"Well," he said, searching for words I could understand, "you're going to have a surprise soon, but you must wait for it."

This was one of the most important and valuable fortunes I'd ever received at Moonglow. Usually these messages were for adults – often about money, wealth, and love – and simply didn't apply to me. But this was a surprise; this spoke to me and I was filled with excitement.

When it was time to leave, my father went to get our boat-like green Chrysler he had parked down the street. My mother, two sisters, and I waited outside the restaurant's door. I understood that women weren't supposed to walk anywhere to get to a car but were to wait, until the man got it for you. When the car pulled up to the curb, my mother, Connie, and Wendy piled into the Chrysler, but I remained standing by the front door of the restaurant, not wanting to move.

"Come on, honey," urged my mother, with the window rolled down, "time to go." I shook my head vigorously, not able to utter a word for fear of crying.

My father stepped out from behind the big black steering wheel and I knew his coming meant business. With a short fuse, there was no "honey" in his voice. "Marsha, time to go, get in the car," he demanded. I couldn't help it and I started to cry. "What's the matter?" said my dad.

"Well, my fortune," I said between muffled sobs. "If I leave, it won't come true."

"What do you mean?" my dad asked in a patient voice.

"The fortune said I have a surprise coming, but I have to wait, so if I leave, I may not get the surprise," I said, with tears streaming down my face. To my astonishment, my father burst into laughter, his fairly slim shoulders bobbing up and down, which meant it was really funny.

"Those fortunes aren't real. They don't really come true, they're just things people make up for fun," he said, smiling and exchanging knowing glances with my mom sitting in the front seat. "Let's go home now, Marsha."

I sulked into the back of the Chrysler to sit on the hump between Wendy and Connie, feeling silly and so much younger than everyone else in my family.

The moon lost a bit of its glow that evening.

Chapter 5
A Mother's Love

IN MY BEDROOM I HAVE A FRAMED 4X6 COLOUR PHOTOGRAPH OF my mother holding me as a baby. In the photo, I am about eight or nine months old, a chubby girl with a round cherubic face, blue eyes, and wisps of soft blond hair that curl off my forehead.

My mother is dressed in her trademark cashmere sweater – red with three-quarter-length sleeves – and she is wearing a pearl necklace that hangs over top the scoop neck. There is a glimmer from her small gold-hoop earrings. I am wearing pale yellow corduroy overalls that snap at the waist, with a soft, long-sleeved light blue jersey-knit shirt underneath. You can see my mother from the waist up and I am pressed against her body, looking out. We are cheek to cheek, engaged in an embrace.

There are so many things I don't know about Mommy. I don't know what made her laugh or cry. What was her favourite food, favourite colour? What were her smells, her stories, her sayings? The photograph helps to piece together a woman I don't remember, a person I never knew. All my thoughts about her are shaped by family anecdotes, photographs, and letters. This impaired ability to recall past events is like living with amnesia. It's as if my early years didn't really exist.

I keep this photograph in its brass frame, on my dresser, where I can see it every morning when I wake up and every evening before I go to sleep. It grounds me in the knowledge that I did have a mother who cared for me and loved me.

The image perfectly captures my mother's pure joy and love for me. Her lips, with a shade of coral-red lipstick to match her sweater, are partially open, showing her closed teeth and half-open eyes, in an expression that can only be described as the one you have when you want to eat that baby up. Pure and utter delight. I know that my father took this picture. If you look very closely at the bottom right-hand side of the photograph, there are two swirls of smoke lingering in the air from his cigar, which evoke memories of the sweet, earthy, and rich scent that always announced his presence.

My father was an amateur photographer and took thousands of slides, photos, and movies that he developed himself in a darkroom that he built in our basement. There were times when we were told "Don't open the door to the darkroom!" when my father was in the process of developing pictures because if the door opened during the process, the pictures would be ruined. Sometimes I perched on a stool in the tiny black room that smelled of acrid chemical fumes from the developing fluids and watched as my father developed snapshots of our life. My father's five-foot-six frame was barely discernible in the dark, but in the red glow of the special safe light, I could see him bent over silver rectangular trays of liquid, his normally carefully coifed combover undone as he concentrated on gently moving the white shiny photographic paper in the trays. It seemed like magic to see images slowly emerge within the liquid, like faces of swimmers bubbling up from beneath lake water. Most of the memories I have of my mother are built around these images.

Connie found copies of letters my mother had written to her brother Stanley, who lived in California. My mother, Betty, was the eldest of four siblings, the only girl among three boys: Stanley, John, and David. In a letter dated March 29, 1957, my mother wrote to Stanley from the hospital: *Well our third little girl was born on March 27th and weighed 7 lbs. 13½ oz. She is so far, unnamed. We were so sure it was a boy. However, she's very sweet and we are thrilled! It's quite strange having a little baby after so many years. Wendy will be 6 in May and both Connie & Wendy can't wait for me to come home from hospital. I imagine they will get a lot of enjoyment from this one.*

Daddy, a macho man who loved hunting, skiing, and talking politics – a "man's man" – had been ready to teach his son the way of the world. He and Mommy had chosen the name Matthew for their third child. He was to be named after Daddy's father, Mottle, following the Jewish tradition of naming children after a deceased family member. He wanted a boy so badly he just thought that, after two girls, surely the next one would be a boy, as if he could will this to happen. My birth shattered these expectations, but reading about my mother's "thrill" at having me makes me feel like I was a welcome addition.

Hungry for details of my mother's life, I devoured these letters, dating from my birth in 1957 until February 1963. Stanley had kept these letters and shared them with Connie, the keeper of the family artifacts. *Marsha is just a doll*, writes my mother in the second page of an undated letter. *We spoil her dreadfully, but she's so pretty you can't help it. She's a little blond butterball with twinkling blue eyes. Children are a lot of work*, she continues, *but we feel that the enjoyment we get from them and recently the companionship can't be duplicated.*

My mother's words and her image captured in photographs affirm my knowledge of and belief in her love. I know in my heart, head, and soul that the riches I received while my mother was alive have carried me through my life's many challenges. For this, I am eternally grateful.

Chapter 6
Mother's Helpers – Daddy's Dalliances

MY MOTHER HAD A SOCIAL CONSCIENCE. SHE READ BETTY FRIEDAN'S 1963 book, *The Feminine Mystique*, which challenged the societal assumption that women could only find fulfillment in their roles as wives and mothers.

In Mommy's copy of the weathered paperback, she left behind highlighted passages and pencilled notes in the margins, indicating how this book spoke to her as she questioned the role of women in society.

As a young adult, I wrote to her best friend, Elenor Schacter, hungry for knowledge of what my mother was like. Elenor mentioned that early in my parents' marriage, before children, my mother and father lived in a bachelor apartment on Duplex, north of Eglinton. It was my mother who supported them then, working for Eaton's at Queen and Yonge in the neckwear and purse department while my father completed his schooling to become a chartered accountant.

When your Dad and my husband, Irving, were members of the Maple Downs Golf Club, your Mom and I went to the Golf Winter School to learn to play golf. We decided that if our husbands were going to play every Saturday and Sunday, we were NOT going to stay home, so we learned to play golf, Elenor wrote in a January 20, 1989, letter.

Elenor affirmed the knowledge that my mother's *interests were toward helping people, particularly women.* After my birth, my mom had a succession of young *unwed mothers* – which was the term used at the time – come and live with us. She provided a home where teenage women were not shamed or judged and could get away for nine months, so their friends and families wouldn't know about their "condition." It also provided my mother with a live-in babysitter so she could play golf, travel, and attend social engagements with my dad.

Connie and Wendy told me we had at least five different women come and stay with us: Pat, Marilyn, Jean, Lois, and Gwen. I only remember Gwen because she became more than a mother's helper, remaining a close friend of our family for many years, ultimately waiting in line to marry Daddy.

As I found out later, when Lois arrived, my mother's brother John, who visited us regularly, took a liking to her and they began dating. John seemed to have a penchant for taking on women with pre-made families. He had previously been married to Bobby, who had a young son. That marriage ended in divorce, after John came home one day to find Bobby had cleared out their entire apartment and gone and married another man in Montreal.

I don't know what Lois's story was, where she came from, how old she was, but John accepted her, pregnancy and all. A caring man, John wanted to create a loving home for Lois and her unborn child, so they married and together they raised a son they named Robert.

In my continued quest for knowledge about my mother, I decided to meet with John when I was in my twenties. He told me how he liked spending time with my mom, saying, "I often dropped into 77 Plymbridge with Robert to visit Betty, which also provided Lois with a much-needed break from the baby." He told me that one day he popped in and was surprised to see my dad's car in the driveway because it was the middle of the workweek. John had taken the day off, as Lois had an appointment she had to attend. He walked in, calling out his name, "Gil?" to no answer. "Betty?" he tried. Still no answer. He'd seen the car, so he knew someone was home, and he began looking around. He heard some noise from their downstairs bedroom, so he walked in unannounced, with baby Robert in tow.

Lois and my father were in bed together.

The telling of this story to me took place many years after the fact, long after Lois and John's marriage had ended, but the lingering anger, betrayal, and grief were still evident in John's retelling of events. I have no way of knowing if the sex was consensual or if Lois was a young, powerless woman who found herself in a position where she couldn't say no.

I do know that what happened with Lois wasn't an isolated event. He'd slept with Gwen and I'm sure there were others. My mother, in an attempt to be altruistic and support pregnant teenagers was an unknown accomplice in supplying my father with easy access to unattached young women.

I guess you could say he helped himself to the mother's helpers..

Chapter 7
Button Nose

MIRI, MY GRANDFATHER SAM'S SECOND WIFE, USED TO CALL ME "button nose." I remember Sam and Miri coming for visits both before and after Mommy died. I don't remember if I called my mother's father "Grandpa" or "Zayde," the traditional Jewish name for a grandfather. I just knew him as Sam.

My mother's mother, Molly, lived apart from Sam for many years. She was sick with asthma and decided to move to Arizona to improve her health. Molly said the air was better there. Clearly something did stink in their home. My mom was a teenager when her mother abandoned her and her three younger brothers. I never knew Molly, and I'm not sure if she died or they divorced, but Sam ended up marrying Miri Moss, a Jewish woman who had converted to Catholicism. She was a divorced woman who had emigrated from England to Canada during the Second World War and came with her young son, Paul. My uncle John said Miri was somehow related to Stirling Moss, the famous race car driver. She was a fast driver and seemed exotic to me, so this connection seemed fitting.

Sam and Miri visited us driving their big white convertible with the top down, their tires screeching to a stop in the driveway to announce their arrival. Daddy prepared for their visits by removing all the alcohol from the teak liquor cabinet that divided the living room from the dining room. We only used the fancy living room when guests came over. It was in the same room as the dining room but was a separate sitting area. Furnished with light lime-green patterned couches, two gold wingback chairs, and white broadloom, it was a special room and we were usually dressed up when we sat in there.

Perched on the rectangular matching teak side table beside the couch was a beautiful geisha doll dressed in a full-length pink-satin flowered kimono. I marvelled at this figurine that Daddy had brought back from Japan after a business trip. I was told only to "Look – don't touch." I was desperate to play with the white-faced doll who had real black hair arranged in a loose bun. I would sometimes sneak into the living room, open the black lacy-patterned wrought-iron doors from the hallway, the mantra of "Keep the doors shut to the living room" in my head. When no one was around, I felt the doll's silky kimono, touched her hair, and wondered at the little pack on her back and the perfectly formed fan she held in her white-gloved hand.

Daddy had bought kimonos from Japan for Connie, Wendy, and me. There is a photograph of the three of us standing in the backyard, lined up by our birth order, each wearing our robes, the competing colours and patterns distracting from the image of our forced smiles.

"Hi, Gil, how ya doing?" Sam bellowed out when he entered the living room. "You got anything to drink?" which seemed rhetorical because he immediately opened the liquor cabinet, searching for a beverage.

Sam was always wearing a black suit when he visited. He had a greasy look about him. His sparse black hair was combed back from his head with some kind of Brylcreem or gel for men. He was always kind of hunched over. He had dark, narrow, shifty eyes and a huge beak-like nose. There was something not right about Sam, and we all just knew not to trust him. Mommy made sure that none of us girls were ever left alone with him, which definitely contributed to our sense of wariness.

One time, Connie and Wendy were in the backyard with Sam, showing him the new dog kennel Daddy had built on the bank of the river. We always had a pet dog in our home. Daddy trained the dogs to hunt with him and thought they would be spoiled if they slept inside, so he designed a large fenced-in kennel with a heated doghouse where they would sleep every night. While the three of them were viewing this caged enclosure, Wendy noticed Sam's hand touching Connie's blouse, coming dangerously close to her breasts. Wendy, ever the brave and forthright one, yelled out, "What are you doing?" and gave him a good push down into the wild ravine below, causing him to land in the pile of dog turds that were a result of the weekly kennel cleaning.

Miri was also always dressed in black. It seemed she only owned one dress or else she had many versions of this same black dress. It was made out of a scratchy stiff fabric and had a wide shawl collar that barely rested on her shoulders, clearly exposing her ample white bosom. The skirt part of the dress was loose to cover her stomach, but the bottom part was tight and fitted, coming just to the knee to show her long, slender calves. She topped it all off with a huge wide-rimmed black hat that she angled stylishly on her head.

While Sam fumbled in the cupboard for liquor, Miri came up to me and grabbed my nose between her thumb and forefinger. "How's my little button nose?" she slurred in her exotic British accent. It always hurt and I tried to avoid this physical contact, but to no avail. She always said, "You are as cute as a button!"

They never stayed long, since the lack of alcohol was disappointing, and then they zoomed off in their convertible, top down, Miri driving, with one hand holding the steering wheel and the other securing her enormous black hat.

My mother was certainly not raised in an idyllic household. From her letter to her brother Stan, dated July 5, 1958: *Dad and Miri were here a couple of weeks ago. You know Miri is a Catholic? She's as big as a house but seems to have calmed down considerably. Daddy, on the other hand, seems much worse. He's very thin and frail looking and drinks far too much. Every time I see him he reeks from liquor. He's crazy about our kids and just can't contain himself when he's with them. Miri is terribly jealous of his affection for them, and so there we are. You see the picture?*

The picture is a little foggy, but I have always wondered whether Sam, or Miri, or both of them, had some kind of history of sexual abuse – as victims or offenders, or both. I googled Miri's son, Paul Vereshack, and what popped up was two and half pages about Paul and his questionable practice as a psychiatrist treating patients using sexual touch therapy. He had authored a book titled *Help Me – I'm Tired of Feeling Bad*. An excerpt from his personal biography for the book, written when he was sixty-four years old, states: "*During those childhood years…I struggled with a mother who was deeply hurt within herself. This struggle added greatly to my other problems and is frankly too private for this particular journal. Suffice it to say that my family life was chaotic in many significant ways. My step-father simply did not have the strength to cope with what he found on his plate.*"

They say that trauma is intergenerational and what doesn't get worked out by one generation will be passed on to the next. How many people are walking around affected by the trauma that seems to have existed in my mother's family? Was my mother ever sexually abused? Was choosing my father, a man who was unfaithful, an unconscious choice, something familiar from her past? I will never know the answer to any of these questions. While Connie, Wendy, and I experienced grief at the loss of our mother, none of us suffered familial sexual abuse nor did we have any substance abuse addictions. The strong attachment and unconditional love Mommy gave us in our childhood carried us through and broke this cycle. The abandonment she must have felt when her mother left her children to live in Arizona was a different kind of loss than what we felt when Mommy died. Still, it is curious how we were all motherless daughters.

Sam and Miri were the only grandparents I knew. Daddy's father, Mottle, died before I was born and his mother, Fanny, died soon after I was born. Like my friend Leigh always says, "You get what you get."

Chapter 8
Grief

I HAVE NO MEMORY OF MY MOTHER'S FUNERAL. WHAT I DO RECALL is Daddy reading two letters from two different women who received my mother's corneas after an organ transplant. Not really understanding about science and transplanting body parts, my belief was that my mother had donated her eyes so that some other women could see. Everyone talked about this as selfless and yet it was also a little contentious since Jews are not supposed to desecrate their bodies upon death. However, if you wanted to give away some parts to help others, you had God's blessing. We were Reform Jews, which meant that you could pretty much do and eat anything and still call yourself Jewish. I thought my mother might need her eyes. Grown-ups were telling me my "mother was looking down on me." So how exactly was she going to see me without her eyes? I also wondered if there were two women walking around who now partly looked like my mother, each with one of her dark brown eyes.

Other than my father walking around inside the house with sunglasses on, there were no visible signs of grieving in our household. Photographs of my mother were put away. The oil painting that hung in the hall – of my mother in a gold-fabric wingback chair, her arm draped along the back while she sat in her green flowing skirt and green and white patterned blouse – disappeared, leaving a telltale faded yellow square behind on the wall.

My friend Susan Stinson called on the telephone and asked me to come over to her house to play the week my mother died. I wanted to go but I also felt an ache and pain that I couldn't explain.

"I can't come," I said to Susan.

"Why not?" she asked.

The three words, *my mother died*, could not come out of my mouth. It was as if my throat had received that freezing you get at the dentist and a numbness larger than life had overcome my ability to say those words. "I just can't come" is all I could muster before hanging up the phone.

Nobody talked to me about grief, dying, how to cope, what to do next. The messages I received in my world were to not talk about my mother and carry on. Everyone I knew had a mother and I had never even thought it possible that someone so large in my life could simply disappear.

I went back to my grade one classroom at York Mills Public School after being away for a week after Mommy died, entering the class with a sense that everyone knew my mother had died but not a word was uttered. My teacher Miss Donald, who was tall, wore her black hair in a French bun, and always wore shimmery blouses with long attached bows at the neckline, was overly sweet and kind to me, touching me on my shoulder and using a tender voice, yet the whispers and stares I felt behind my back were like those no-see-um bugs that come out in the summer in rural Ontario. You can hardly see those tiny gnats, but you can always feel their presence.

I tried to find others who were like me and took some refuge in watching TV shows like *My Three Sons*, where the three teenage boys had a father, a male housekeeper named Uncle Charley and no mother around. In *Make Room for Daddy* and *The Andy Griffith Show*, the men were widowers like my dad, who had to juggle career and family. *The Sound of Music* and *Mary Poppins* were my all-time favourite films, giving me hope that perhaps a nanny who looked like Julie Andrews would come and make everything all right. I got my hair cut like Julie

Andrews. My hair was short, straight, and light blond and I had a small combover from a part on the side with bangs that feathered on my forehead. If Julie did show up, I could pass for her daughter.

I also turned to literature to find motherless daughters. There was *Madeline*, the little French girl who appeared to have no parents at all but had a pretty good life in her boarding school with all the other girls, although the ending always seemed a bit grim: "That's all there is, there isn't any more." There were *Babar*, *Cinderella*, *Snow White*, and when I got older *Heidi*. I discovered an abundance of stories of children without mothers and I think this bibliotherapy helped me try to cope with and normalize my grief.

Connie, who was fifteen years old when our mother died, and Wendy, who was twelve, were so much older than me and found their own ways of coping with the unspoken trauma. Connie was thrust into the role of "wife and mother," picking up my father's dry cleaning and doing the grocery shopping in the big green Chrysler, even though she didn't have a driver's licence yet. Wendy had oodles of friends and used her new unexpected freedom to try everything: smoking, drinking, and listening to rock and roll with a different crowd every weekend.

It wasn't long before my father decided he needed someone to take care of the household with three growing daughters, but, unlike *My Three Sons*, it clearly wasn't going to be an Uncle Charley

Chapter 9
Domestic Dilemmas

WE SHARED OUR HOME AND LIFE WITH A SERIES OF WOMEN. SOME of them my dad paid as housekeepers and some he married.

A live-in housekeeper named Mrs. Szabo, a Hungarian ball of fire, was the first to arrive. In her mid-forties, she had wild, unkempt short dark brown hair that always stood up straight, as if she'd just watched a horror movie. She described herself as a good cook and we were eager to taste her signature dish that she boasted about: chicken paprikash. However, this dish soon lost its lustre when it became our regular evening meal. Often wearing a white terrycloth robe that she tied tightly around her thick waist, Mrs. Szabo – I never knew her first name – entered my father's bedroom on the main floor every morning to do callisthenic exercises with him. Mrs. Szabo had her own bedroom on the second floor, while the three of us girls squished into the other bedroom. My father was athletic, priding himself on keeping in shape. He always maintained a weekly exercise regimen, either jogging or doing a workout routine in his bedroom.

Once Mrs. Szabo found out that he exercised regularly, she waltzed in to his bedroom in her terrycloth robe every morning. Daddy didn't invite Mrs. Szabo to join him, and he didn't like it one bit. It was hilarious to walk by my father's bedroom in the morning and see the two of them bouncing up and down, doing jumping jacks together. Daddy didn't know what to do or how to say no. It was ironic that my controlling, demanding father had an absolute inability to have any authority over any housekeeper he hired. He started and managed his own very successful chartered accountant company, yet he became powerless in his own home with the hired help.

One evening, Mrs. Szabo's Hungarian boyfriend came to visit, a diminutive man who was balding and spoke very little English. When he parked his car on our front lawn, my father was furious, and this must have given him the adrenalin he needed to fire Mrs. Szabo. I can still see the poor bumbling fellow with his hat placed over his stomach, bowing and repeating, "But you said to park on the front." Apparently where he was from, parking your car on the front lawn was the thing to do.

Helen was hired in a hurry.

A rotund Caribbean woman with a smile that warmed your insides, Helen brought some joy and laughter into our motherless home. Unlike Mrs. Szabo, Helen was only referred to by her first name. She took over the second bedroom at the top of the stairs and it seemed that Connie, Wendy, and I were destined to share a bedroom together forever.

Our bedroom, at the end of the long hall upstairs, didn't really have room for three beds. Connie slept on the left side of the rectangular room, with her bed facing the dormer window. Wendy was on the right, across from Connie, with a matching dormer window. The two sides also had identical sloping ceilings that slanted away from their windows. Apart from that, the two sides of the room couldn't have looked more different. Connie's walls were clean and pristine, with only the forest-green paint evident. Wendy, on the other hand, had her walls plastered with posters of the Beatles, with no evidence of green paint anywhere. A black-and-white collage of the fab four – George, Ringo, John, and Paul – covered every speck of space on her wall. Paul, of course, was her favourite. Those doe eyes stared back at you day and night from the large colour posters of him that were taped to cover the sloped ceiling.

Since I was the youngest sibling, I had little or no wall space. Actually, I had no space at all. I slept on a textured, faded red-cloth daybed that was barely big enough to fit me. Wendy and Connie had twin beds with matching white chenille bedspreads. My daybed was hard, with a steel tube at the top. Making my "bed" involved turning it back into a two-seater couch. The one advantage to my small area was that it butted against a cupboard that opened into a crawl space in the attic. When I opened the door and entered into this compartment, it became a magical room for me. No matter that it was musty-smelling and the floor was covered in soft pieces of grey-black insulation, this was my special private getaway, where I could escape with my dolls. The room scared me a bit with its darkness and silence, but I told myself that just made it more of an adventure.

While Connie and Wendy were independent, I was a seven-year-old, still needing care after school. Lunchtime I managed on my own. I was what people called a "latch-key kid." With a key literally hung around my neck, I walked home from public school and made my own lunch. I had time to watch *The Flintstones* on TV and then head back for the thirty-minute walk to school. It was a lonely and desolate time, and I was always glad when Susan Stinson invited me to her house for lunch, where red-headed Mrs. Stinson rustled up peanut butter and jam sandwiches or tuna and cheese melts for her four children: Susan, Carol, and Joanne (who were all redheads), and Kathy, the youngest (who was blond). Their red hair branded them as a family, and I wondered if Kathy felt a little left out. I loved going down the road to their house, where there was always lots of noise and activity. It felt so different from my quiet and orderly empty house.

Since we were in school all day, Helen had time to clean the house, do the laundry, and prepare our dinner. We had now graduated from chicken paprikash to jerk chicken.

Maybe my dad took some shortcuts when he hired Helen and didn't check her references, but out of the blue something just snapped inside her.

In the middle of a cold wintery night in January, Helen dialled 911 to report that my father was strangling her. "Mr. Barrett is trying to kill me," she yelled at the top of her lungs into the phone. "You need for come now," she screamed.

My father, woken from sleep, rushed upstairs to Helen's room.

Helen was standing beside her bed, the black phone receiver to her ear, with its umbilical-like cord stretched to capacity, holding a white bedsheet that was tied in a knot.

"I have proof," she screamed to the police at the other end of the receiver. "My bedsheet is tied in a knot, where he tried to strangle me. I need to get out of this house. You need for come now."

Not knowing what to do, my father went downstairs and spoke to the police on the other phone. Daddy, a well-connected man, happened to know the chief of police, so he dropped his name.

"Yeah, this is Gil Barrett here and I know James Mackey and I'm telling you that our housekeeper Helen seems to be having some kind of a fit. I am definitely not trying to strangle her. She just woke up and started screaming. I am going to need some help here, could you send someone around?"

Within minutes two male police officers arrived in the middle of the night and came upstairs to Helen's bedroom. They were overdressed in their big black boots, coats, and hats compared to Helen, who was sitting on the edge of her bed wearing a thin cotton short-sleeved lavender nightie with a scooped white-lace neckline.

"You're going to have to come with us, Helen," one of the officers said. While she had committed no crime, my father had convinced the officers (it didn't take much convincing) that it wasn't safe to have Helen in our house, as he was worried for his children's safety. They were going to take her to some kind of psychiatric hospital.

Suddenly Helen, who had been pleading to get out of this house where her boss was trying to kill her, didn't want to leave. She hung on to the doorknob and the wall, yelling, "I'm not going nowhere."

The police conferred with my dad and they made the decision that she'd have to be forcefully removed. The kinder, gentler officer asked Helen where her coat was, so she could cover up. Helen pointed to a stuffed chair and there lay a thin nylon-quilted lavender housecoat with white lace at the collar and sleeves that matched her nightie. Helen put on the housecoat, doing up the four big purple buttons that went down the front. It all seemed to be going well. She went downstairs and the police opened the front door. The cold evening air entered the house and I couldn't help thinking, Aren't they going to put a coat on her?

Helen grabbed the doorframe with both hands and let out a howl: "I'm not going nowhere. You have to drag me out!"

The officers grabbed Helen under the arms, one at each side, and did just that. She resisted all the way, and my last image of Helen was of her bare black legs trailing through the white snow, dressed only in her lavender nightie and housecoat.

When I woke late in the morning, I said to Daddy that it'd been hard to get to sleep because I was scared. "It felt like someone came into my room last night," I said.

"Yeah, that was me," he said. "I was just checking on you to see if you were okay. Actually, Helen came back last night, as there was no hospital that would take her. The police tried several places and they couldn't find any reason to admit her. I didn't know what to do, I felt bad for her, so she came back for the night."

"Is she still here?" I asked with trepidation.

"No, she's left on her own. A friend of hers came to pick her up this morning."

While part of me thought my father was feeble as he had now let two housekeepers have authority over him, another side of me saw kindness, and it was hard for me to reconcile the two feelings.

I was still waiting for a nanny like Mary Poppins to show up, someone who would make everything all right, or perhaps one like Maria Von Trapp, who Daddy might marry.

Chapter 10
Camp Oconto

"A MONTH IN THE WILDERNESS WILL BE GOOD FOR YOU AND YOU'LL learn how to swim," Daddy assured me while we drove to Yorkdale Mall to catch the bus that would take me to Camp Oconto.

When I was four or five years old, Daddy had decided that the best way to teach me to swim was the sink-or-swim method. We had a thirty-two-foot cabin cruiser called *Beverley the III* – the name was of no significance, we bought it that way. We kept the boat docked at Lefroy Harbour, on Lake Simcoe. We often went up as a family to take the boat out on the lake, anchoring it for the day to swim and have lunch near Fox Island. One day, my father strapped a bright orange life jacket on me and told me I was going to learn to swim. His lessons involved no instruction. My father picked me up, hung me over the side of the boat, six feet from the water, and threw me in. I felt panic and fear as I plunged feet first into the cold deep lake. I popped up coughing water, crying and terrified. This experience backfired: rather than teaching me to swim, it solidified my fear of water and I never so much as dipped a toe into a puddle after that.

Connie and Wendy were going to camp for the whole summer and I was going for July. "But I don't want to go for a whole month," I pleaded in the middle of a frosty January afternoon while Daddy filled out the forms to secure our spots.

"You can only go for one month or two at Camp Oconto. That's it. Your sisters will be there and you're gonna love it. You'll go canoeing, camping, and make all kinds of girlfriends."

The all-girls camp was a rugged retreat north of Kingston. You slept in tents with floorboards, used outhouses, and went on canoe trips where you portaged and trekked through the woods, cooking your food over a campfire. With no school during the summer months, my father needed to house us somewhere, and camp seemed like the perfect opportunity to "help build our character and learn valuable skills." There was nothing to worry about.

> "Have you been to Camp Oconto?
> On the shores of Eagle Lake
> Where the red canoes
> Will chase the blues
> On the camping trips you take"

So went the camp song, still ingrained in my memory like an earworm. I was seven years old and had never been away from home.

I was in one of the youngest camper groups, the Tadpole section, or Tads as we came to be known, and shared a cabin with three other girls my age. Only the seniors, like Connie and Wendy, were in tents, and they were in a different part of the camp that I never went to. I didn't even know how to get there. I rarely saw them.

We called all the counsellors by their last names and each cabin had their own counsellor; ours was Miss Abrams. We all wore uniforms of cotton brown/taupe shorts with matching pullover shirts that had a V-neck and no buttons. When we got together in the dining hall for our meals, it looked like we were part of some kind of religious cult. On Sundays, we wore the same style of uniform but in white. Each section of the camp gathered in the middle of the woods for "chapel." It was a spiritual experience, with rough-hewn logs for seats in the middle of the forest, which smelled of pine and a heady mixture of wildflowers. The birds sang a morning song and sunlight streamed through the leafy green branches, creating a calm and peaceful time that worshipped the beauty of nature. The so-called "service" was non-denominational and it was a quiet, thoughtful, and reflective homily that emphasized giving thanks to whatever or whoever you believed in. While it was not focused on any one religion, the concept of Sunday service clearly reflected that most of the campers were Christian. Jews were in short supply.

Other than the one hour of "rest time" each day in our cabins after lunch, we were busy every second: arts and crafts, archery, team games, canoeing, knot tying, hiking, and swimming. The bell tolled at 7:00 a.m. "Rise and shine campers!" said Miss Abrams every morning, ensuring we were on time for the flag-raising ceremony when we all chanted "Salutation to the Sun." After eating breakfast in the dining hall, we headed down to the dock for the morning swim lesson. It was terrifying.

When Miss Abrams called out "Swim time!" with vim and vigour in her voice, my stomach turned into one of those figure-eight knots that we had learned in rope-tying class.

On the first day of camp, the wind was whistling at the dock with whitecaps forming as far as the eye could see. All the Tads broke off into small groups, our warm thick towels wrapped around our thin shivering bodies, while we were put into divisions to test our swimming abilities. "Jump in," urged my swim instructor, Miss White. I lingered and watched as one by one each of the Tadpoles in my group hopped in, living up to the expectation of our name. I, on the other hand, stood numb and frozen like one of those people I had learned about from Pompeii whose bodies were hardened into stone, captured doing everyday activities after the volcano erupted.

"I can't swim," I said to Miss White, my teeth chattering.

"Can you get into the water?"

What to do? The pressure to go along was intense, yet the panic and bile that was rising in my throat at the thought of getting into that dark, deep, freezing water outweighed my compliance.

Miss White got down on her knees, looked me in the eye, and said, "Don't worry, Marsha. We'll teach you how to swim. That's what camp is all about."

She blew the silver whistle that hung around her neck, waved her hand, and another counsellor magically popped out of the water like a mermaid. She lifted herself onto the dock, coming over to me all dripping wet with goosebumps on her thick legs.

"Miss Downey is going to work with you in the shallow end, so you can go with her," said Miss White. The kindness and gentleness caught me by surprise. I gratefully followed Miss Downey to the shallow sandy beach area.

Each morning at swim time, Miss Downey and I waded into the water, going a little deeper each day. After about two weeks, when I got in up to my knees, Miss Downey said, "Let's try blowing bubbles." I watched while Miss Downey bent her head into the water, with just her white bathing cap floating on top. A deep, bellowing whale-like sound emerged from her mouth and big mounds of water bubbled up like a motorboat had started. It looked like fun and I did trust Miss Downey. I tried it. The water was silky smooth on my face and I felt like Moses parting the Red Sea, as I created this massive movement of water. I came up to squeals of delight and encouragement. "You did it, Marsha!! Way to go. You were so brave!" said Miss Downey, raising her hand to give me a high five. I beamed with pride at my achievement and for the first time felt at one with the water without fear.

"We can add this to the swimming success wall!" said Miss Downey. The swimming success wall was a chart in the Tads main lodge that listed each camper's name and swimming milestones. All the other girls had multiple checks in the columns identifying that they had mastered skills such as: jumping in, treading water, frog kick. I, meanwhile, had no checkmarks. I was relieved to have finally earned one beside blowing bubbles, especially because it was Visitors Day next weekend and Daddy could now see I had made progress.

I was homesick and was looking forward to his visit at the two-week mark of camp. He brought a care package full of Archie comics, jujubes, Lik-M-Aid, potato chips, and cream soda. It felt good to have a taste of home. I walked Daddy around the camp, proudly showing him my cabin, introducing him to my friends, Miss Abrams, and the campgrounds. We got to the Tadpoles' main lodge and he saw the swimming success wall.

"What's this?" he asked.

Miss Abrams explained about "our wall of accomplishment," and I waited expectantly as I saw Daddy looking for my name.

"What the hell? You have one checkmark beside your name for blowing bubbles? That's it? Look what all these other girls have done! Jesus, I pay a fortune for this camp and all you're doing is blowing bubbles?" His shoulders began to hump up and down in that familiar movement, as he started to laugh.

I could feel the heat begin in my neck as it rapidly climbed to my face, making my redness a visible marker of my shame and embarrassment. I was mortified that my father talked like this in front of everyone. Suddenly my accomplishment seemed laughable and my pride at blowing bubbles was little more than being recognized for drooling in the water. Miss Downey was, like her name, a soft feathery landing, but in reality I hadn't really accomplished anything significant.

The crowd of parents and campers in the room suddenly went quiet. Miss Abrams closed her open mouth and tried to say something positive. I don't remember what she said because I couldn't hear with the buzzing of humiliation in my ears. I guess I wasn't going to come home a swimmer after all.

Chapter 11
The Strains

IT AMAZES ME HOW WELL PEOPLE SUIT THEIR NAMES. DO NEW-borns grow into their names, or do parents have an uncanny sense of that child's personality very early on? It's likely both, nature and nurture. Viola and Bob Strain suited their names perfectly. Viola spoke in a high register, like the four-stringed instrument, and was wiry, always moving and talking at a fast pace. Her husband, Bob, on the other hand, moved with extreme slowness. He had more to move around. He was an obese man, weighing over two hundred pounds, with a pin head and a close-shaved grey crewcut. The letters in his name could stand for *box office bomb*. Our family nicknamed him "the glump" – indicative of his lethargy and dour personality.

After going through the bad experiences with Mrs. Szabo and Helen, my father thought that hiring a married couple would solve many of our problems. The concept was that Viola could do all the housekeeping and cooking, and Bob could do yard maintenance and other "man type" work. They had each other for company, which might prevent any issues of loneliness or craziness.

I watched while our basement filled up with an upholstered couch and matching chair set, a veneer coffee table, and a television. The Strains were going to "live in" and the basement was to become their living room. The upstairs bedroom was now going to belong to Viola and Bob. Being only nine years old, I had no sense of their age; they just seemed old to me and I never questioned why a married couple didn't have their own home and why they'd want to live and work with our family. My father said they had a grown son who had his own family somewhere.

Connie enrolled in nursing school, so she'd made the break from home and was living in residence in downtown Toronto. I graduated from my daybed into a real bed across from Wendy. The only time I even remember seeing Wendy was late at night when she'd slip into her side of the room, after having returned from one of her parties.

Viola was a take-charge kind of woman: our kitchen was soon in shipshape and we enjoyed a variety of meals every evening. A fourth-generation Canadian, she cooked meat loaf, mashed potatoes and peas, pot pies, stews, and other hearty dishes that kept Bob and the rest of us high in caloric content. Bob and Viola always ate dinner with Daddy, Wendy, and me in the more formal dining room with the oval teak table and matching chairs. I didn't like this because Viola sat at the head of the table, dishing out the food in a spot and a role that I thought was reserved only for a mother. I don't think my father liked this setup either, since Viola, while taking up physical space, also chatted all through dinner about her events of the day. My father, weary after work, resigned himself to this situation, as he had with all the other housekeepers, and gnawed on his chicken bone that was covered in Shake'n Bake breadcrumbs.

It seemed that Bob was having trouble keeping his end of the bargain in terms of doing the yard work. Our lawn was not mowed regularly, the gardens were unkempt, and Bob had many physical ailments that were keeping him from getting away from the TV in the basement. Bob also had a lot of complaints about my father, our family, and how things were in our household. He was especially critical of my many inabilities.

"How come a big kid like you doesn't know how to ride a bike? You should be out there riding a bike, climbing trees," bellowed Bob.

"You don't even know how to swim," he admonished.

It was true. I hadn't learned how to do all the typical things the other kids my age were doing. I was fearful. My fear was rooted both in reality and in feeling wildly un-mothered, with no soft place to land if disaster happened.

Bob, of course, didn't know the roots of my fear. All he saw was a "scaredy-cat" and an inept father who wasn't doing his job.

Sitting around the dining-room table over dinner one night, Bob kept going at me – living up to his name of being a glump – about "how I should be out climbing trees" and how he had a notion to teach me how to ride a bike.

"I don't see you outside trimming the trees or cutting the grass and maybe that's why you're so fat!" I said with conviction, summoning up a courage that went well beyond my athletic inabilities. I knew I had crossed a line, but it felt good. I had tapped into something, an anger, that made me feel powerful and confident.

My father didn't admonish me, and it felt like I had spoken something that the rest of my family was thinking, like that children's story by Hans Christian Andersen, *The Emperor's New Clothes*. Bob pushed his chair back from the table, grunted loudly, and stormed off downstairs to his TV. Viola, silenced for the first time ever, busied herself with clearing the table.

The next day, my father taught me how to ride a bike.

Viola had plenty to say to Daddy about my rude and disrespectful behaviour toward Bob. She was always his spokesperson. The incident did, however, help to raise the issue of the lack of yard work being done by Bob and soon after, he started mowing the grass.

When I rode past Bob on my bike, while he trimmed our hedges, he looked at me sideways and grinned, confident that his outburst had had an impact on my father's behaviour. But so had mine.

Chapter 12
B61

BOTH OF MY PARENTS WERE AVID GOLFERS, AND BEFORE I WAS born they had difficulty finding a club to join since no Jews were allowed at any of the golf clubs in Toronto. In 1954, my father and ten other men met at the Pride of Israel Hall to create the Maple Downs Golf Club in Oak Ridges Moraine. Designed by William Mitchell, this golf club still exists today.

Later, during the 1960s, Jews were being allowed into private clubs. Wealthy Jewish families like the Kofflers, who started Shoppers Drug Mart, and the Creeds, of Creed Furs, were neighbours of ours in "the valley" and because they could contribute a fair bit financially to golf clubs, ski clubs, and other private enclaves, the gentiles started to see a few token Jews as an asset.

Daddy joined the Donalda Club because it was inclusive and had a beautiful dining room where he could take business clients out for dinner. The club was like a majestic country home, situated far from the road with tall trees and beautiful gardens surrounding a mansion that looked like something out of *Gone with the Wind*. It had large white pillared columns evenly spaced across the grand front porch.

"The club," as we came to call it, was in Don Mills, a suburban neighbourhood that seemed far from our house. In the summer, I often took the bus there with a girlfriend so we could spend the day lounging by the outdoor pool. There were only certain girlfriends I could take with me. They had to be friends whose parents let them take the bus on their own. I was only ten or eleven years old and most parents didn't allow this. Julie Connolly was often my companion to the club. Julie had no father. He had died when she was young, so we had the loss of a parent in common. Julie's mother seemed very old and there were very few rules in their house. I knew Julie's family didn't have much money because they had no furniture in their living room and the carpet was threadbare. The only cost in going to the club was the bus fare, so Julie was always a first choice in accompanying me. It was odd to take the bus to a country club. I felt out of place walking down the long winding road with my swimsuit in a plastic bag while fancy cars passed us driving down the well-manicured garden-lined lane.

Julie and I ordered a "free" lunch. It seemed free because Daddy had given me the account number, B61. This magic number was all that was needed to sit under the umbrellas on the patio and order a burger and fries. I sometimes travelled to the club by myself. With Daddy at work, I'd be hanging around on hot summer days with nothing to do, so I thought I might as well lounge on my own by a pool. There were never any kids my age by themselves at the pool and I always felt that I was breaking some regulation by being there all alone. I'm sure I probably was. Big signs that read "Children cannot be left unattended" reinforced this feeling, so I sat in a lounge chair that was strategically placed near a family.

Our family went out for dinner to the club about once a month because my father said he had to "use up his food account." I never understood what this meant but loved going there for dinner. We all dressed up and I ordered my favourite meal of roast beef. I never ordered anything else. It came to be a family joke. "I wonder what Marsha will order?" my sister Wendy would say, teasing me. I didn't understand the sarcasm and always responded with enthusiasm, "I'm going to have roast beef!"

Viola and Bob Strain came with us to our dinners at the club. It struck me as odd. I couldn't name why it was odd, but even as a child I could sense the class difference and had a feeling that most people eating in the Donalda Club dining room were not sitting at their tables with their housekeeper and gardener. There was something just too loud about Viola's voice and flowered print dress that stood out in the quiet, subdued dining room.

One evening, Daddy, Viola, Bob, Connie, Wendy, and I were on our way out for dinner to the club. My father backed up the car from the garage and Connie and Wendy got in the front seat with him. Those were the days when you could fit three people in the front seat. Viola, Bob, and I were to get in the back. Viola crossed her arms and refused to get in the car.

"What's the matter, Viola?" queried my dad.

"I refuse to ride in the back seat of the car. The children should be in the back seat, and Bob and I should be in the front!" she proclaimed in a loud and demanding voice. "Especially since we're going to the Donalda Club for dinner. I don't want to get out in front of the club from the back seat."

Exasperated, my father turned to Connie and Wendy and asked if they would mind moving. Wendy – a middle child who had strength, conviction, and courage – said, "No, we want to ride in the front with our dad."

"Well, then, I'm not going," said Viola, epitomizing every ounce of her surname.

My father, chronically lacking conviction and courage as an employer of domestic help, succumbed to Viola's request. Connie and Wendy moved to the back seat and off we went to the club, Bob squished beside my dad and Viola's head held high while she gazed out the coveted front passenger window.

Chapter 13
Carol

"I have good news," announced Daddy on a sunny Saturday morning in January as Connie, Wendy, and I sat around the kitchen table for a brunch of bagels, lox, and cream cheese. Connie was eighteen and still living in nursing residence, Wendy was fifteen, and I was nine.

"I'm getting married!" he said jubilantly.

Daddy had been dating Carol for a very brief time. An attractive young woman in her early thirties, Carol had a slender build and mid-length auburn hair that came to her chin, flipping up at the ends, in the style of the day. My father, who was forty-four, didn't have to go far to find his new wife. Carol worked as Daddy's secretary in his office. She was a gentile and had never been married before.

All three of us had different reactions to the impending marriage. Connie, who wasn't living at home, was happy for my father and likely relieved, since she wouldn't have to live with Carol and could now be released of her remaining household and parenting duties. Connie often had the task of looking after me and playing the "mother" figure, a role that was beyond her years and capability.

Wendy responded negatively. "I hope she won't be telling me what to do," she said, worried that adding a stepmother to the household might put a damper on her currently unlimited freedom.

I was craving a mother figure. I liked Carol's quiet ways and was looking forward to having some sense of stability and sanity in our family. I was often lonely and thought that having a young and pretty stepmother around would be a good thing.

We all mumbled our congratulations while thinking about the impact this new relationship was going to have on our own lives.

The best part of this news was that the Strains would now be leaving. Not knowing how to get rid of them, I almost think that my father found a wife so he could avoid having to deal with firing Viola and Bob.

The following week, when we were sitting around the dinner table eating Viola's homemade shepherd's pie and a wedge of iceberg lettuce with French dressing, my father broke the news of his upcoming nuptials to Viola and Bob.

Viola looked at Wendy and me for signs of how we were registering this news. Our faces were blank, having had a week to digest and discuss the concept of a stepmother.

"You don't seem surprised about this. How do you feel?" Viola asked us in a tight, high-pitched voice, her lips pinched.

We hunched our shoulders and muttered that we were happy for our dad, sensing that Viola didn't share any positive emotion about this.

"Is this the first time you're hearing this news?"

"Oh, no, Daddy told us last week," said Wendy.

"Whaaat?" cried Viola loudly. "You told your children this news before you told Bob and me? What kind of man are you?" she demanded. "We should have been the first to know! It also affects us in a very large way."

For the first time, I saw my dad respond with assertiveness.

"My children come first, Viola. I'm your employer and your reaction is unexpected and unreasonable," Daddy said. "I'm giving you lots of notice, so you'll have time to find another position."

Viola huffed away in her fuzzy white mule slippers, dragging Bob with her. He said nothing but looked glumpy. We could all hear her down in the basement yelling nasty things about my father while Bob's TV did a poor job of tuning her out.

Two Strains were going, but another was yet to come.

Chapter 14
A Stepmother

CAROL AND MY FATHER GOT MARRIED IN WINTER AT THE DONALDA Club in a special room that was reserved for weddings. It was a small gathering of only twenty people for dinner at a large U-shaped table. Carol wore a knee-length white brocade dress with a scoop neck and three-quarter-length sleeves. It was very plain and not at all what I was imagining a bride should wear. I was hoping for a white chiffon, organza, or tulle gown that puffed out in many layers, like my Barbie doll fairy-tale wedding dress, which was full of glitter and lace. Perched on top of her perfectly hair-sprayed flip, Carol wore a white satin pillbox hat that reminded me of Jackie Kennedy. I felt special all night because Carol made sure I sat on the other side of her at the big table for dinner. I was the only child there.

Before they got married, Carol went through a rigorous process of converting to Judaism. I don't know if my dad asked her to do this or if Carol had some kind of religious transformation. She didn't seem Jewish at all to me, especially in December when we had a fake white Christmas tree at our house to accommodate her. My dad called it a Chanukah bush and we decorated it with big shiny blue balls. My father said that white and blue were the colours of Israel, so it met the requirements of being Jew…*ish*.

Carol's brother, David, was younger than her and a lot of fun. A tall, thin lanky guy who seemed to fold in on himself when he sat in a chair, he always had a comical joke or story to share. His dark brown hair was plentiful and he had waves of it on his forehead. He also had lots of freckles on his nose, which added to his youthfulness.

Carol's parents were divorced and she had two sets of parents: Phyllis and Bill, and Harold and Lillian. I found this intriguing because Carol had some experience in what it was like to have a stepparent. Phyllis was her real mom and Harold was her real dad. She didn't see Harold and Lillian too much and she seemed to be closer to her stepfather, Bill, than she was to her own mother, Phyllis.

Phyllis looked like a beaver. A rotund woman with no hips, large protruding front teeth, and short hair and glasses, she was always nodding her head up and down like the beaver in the Disney movie *Lady and the Tramp*. When I met Carol's mom and stepdad, she introduced them as Phil and Bill, so I wasn't sure which one was Phil and which one was Bill. I called them Uncle Bill and Aunt Phil and it took me a while to figure it out. I was always mixing up their names, calling them Aunt Bill and Uncle Phil, which made everyone laugh. Bill was a quiet gentle man with an abundance of combed-back straight white hair that was soft like the silk on a cob of corn. He had pink skin and a round face, with twinkly eyes underneath his wire-framed glasses. He reminded me a bit of a clean-shaven Santa Claus.

Phil and Bill were an odd match. She was as loud as he was quiet. Phil seemed to boss Bill around and he never said too much about it. I could tell that Carol loved Bill by the warm, loving glances they exchanged and she always talked about him. I wondered why Bill had chosen Phil, because Lillian, a quiet thoughtful woman, seemed a lot nicer and more his type. Whenever Phil and Bill came over to our house, Phil acted "funny," slurring her words, talking very loudly, and laughing a lot. My father always said he had to hide all the liquor before they came for dinner.

Phil and Bill had a cottage at Port Elgin and I remember going there often with Carol and staying overnight. They had a screened-in porch that overlooked Lake Huron, and we would sit on their white wicker furniture that had yellow and red flowered chintz cushions and play card games like Crazy Eights and Go Fish. Bill taught me how to play Gin Rummy, which sounded very adult-like, and I was proud that I had mastered a game that seemed like poker to me. Bill seemed to have nothing but time and he gave me a lot of it.

Carol also spent a lot of time with me and was the first woman who had been truly kind and nurturing to me since my mother died.

Wendy and Carol fought all the time and Wendy often said, "I hate Carol and wish she would die!" I guess Carol tried to put restrictions on all of Wendy's partying, which had limited success. I wanted my big sister Wendy to see me as cool, so I agreed with her, but really I loved Carol and felt like she had saved me from my loneliness.

One day I was upstairs in the hall, where I had positioned myself by the banister near the stairway so I'd be out of sight, and I called out to Carol, who was on the main floor, "Carol, I want to ask you something." I knew what I was going to ask was important and I wasn't quite sure how to say it and what the response might be. My heart was pounding so loud, I thought she could hear it.

"Yes, what is it, sweetie?" she called up to me from the bottom of the stairs. Trying to sound casual, I wrapped my dry mouth and palpitating heart around the words and said, "Can I call you Mom?"

There was a long silence and I waited for what seemed like an eternity for her to respond. I heard her voice croak and break like someone who was speaking for the first time after waking up in the morning and she said, "Of course you can."

I felt warm inside every part of my body. At last, I had a mother's love.

Chapter 15
The Den

EVEN THOUGH I HAD ASKED CAROL IF I COULD CALL HER MOM, I couldn't actually utter the three-letter word. It was just too hard for me. Somehow it felt I was being disrespectful or forgetting about Mommy and it would upset my father and sisters. I didn't tell anyone that I had asked Carol if I could elevate her to this important role and she never referred to it again when I continued to call her Carol. I respected her for this and it made me love her even more.

Carol and I had settled into a predictable routine. With Connie living away, Wendy gone most of the time, and my dad at the office a lot and also travelling with his work, it was usually just Carol and me who were together before and after school.

On Friday mornings Carol got her hair done at the hairdresser. I loved coming home from school on Fridays and entering the front door to the smell of strongly antiseptic, yet slightly floral hair spray. This reliable weekly ritual gave me comfort and predictability, something I felt I had been lacking in my short ten years of life. Carol didn't get her hair cut every week but got what she called "a wash and wear." When I touched her hair, it didn't seem washed but stiff as a board, with every hair in place, more like wax and wear; however, Carol always held her head a little higher on Fridays and I could see that the wash and wear made her happy.

I so wanted Carol to be happy. Sometimes during the week, Carol didn't brush her hair at all or change out of what she called her housedress, a shapeless flowered cotton dress that zipped up the front. She'd sit in what we called the den in our house and stare at nothing in particular.

The den was my favourite room at 77 Plymbridge. The walls were panelled with tongue-and-groove knotty pine that had a sheen to it. It was a cozy room with two large orange-skirted upholstered chairs that faced each other: one that was stationary and the other that rocked and swivelled. I always wanted to sit in the swivel chair that could swing to watch the television that was nestled in the built-in bookcase or to look out to the backyard. A comfy two-seater hunter-green cloth couch was against the wall facing the fireplace, which was enclosed in glass doors with brass trim. The doors folded out if you wanted to see the gas flame or you could slide small rectangular doors underneath to give heat but keep the doors closed.

Mounted above the fireplace were four long rifles that my dad used to hunt ducks and other wild game. The hunter-green colour of the couch was fitting. People today call these rooms "man caves." I guess this was my father's man cave, complete with firearms.

The den was where we sat when we ordered in Chinese food from Sea-Hi and watched the Disney show after a Sunday of downhill skiing. We would pull out the pine tea wagon with brass wheels that was used as a corner table all week, lift up the extension that turned the table from a rectangle into a square, and load it up with red cardboard boxes decorated with black dragons. Opening the flaps of the cardboard filled the room with the steaming scent of fried food coated with sesame oil, garlic, and ginger. No need for serving dishes or conversation.

The den was where Connie and Wendy always went with their dates so they could "watch TV." We all knew, my father included, that the only thing they were watching was if the thick wooden door to the den opened to reveal them making out on the couch.

The den was also where serious conversations were had (the guns helped to create a solemn tone).

My dad smoked his cigars and pipes in the den. He had a humidor, a dark red wooden square box that smelled like cedar when you opened it, to keep his cigars fresh. It was my job to clean the thin rectangular gold filter that slid inside the humidor lid. I loved both the responsibility and the task of this weekly chore. I was also allowed to soak the filter in my father's downstairs bathroom, which was otherwise forbidden territory.

"Use the upstairs bathroom," my father bellowed if I trespassed.

I wasn't sure why I couldn't use the bathroom on the main floor – which also linked to his bedroom – but whenever I cleaned the filters in one of the double sinks in his bathroom, I rummaged through the drawers, looking for clues to emerge like the tiny bubbles that rose to the surface as I held the filter under the water. I think the connecting bedroom held many mysteries because this was a room that was totally off limits to me.

Much to my father's delight, Carol had taken to smoking a pipe. She enjoyed the taste and smell of tobacco, which was highly unusual for a woman. Daddy found a special pipe for Carol that had a pink bowl with sparkling rhinestones around the rim.

Sometimes, when Carol was sitting in the den wearing her housedress, she was smoking her pink pipe. This seemed better than simply staring at nothing in particular.

Chapter 16
Rituals

ONCE CAROL AND DADDY WERE MARRIED, CAROL WAS NO LONGER my father's full-time secretary at his office, but she did go in sometimes to work and help out when needed. I loved the days when Carol didn't go into work because she was there when I came home after school.

At 4:00 p.m., after the long thirty-minute walk from school to home, I ran to open the black-painted wooden front door and immediately turn the corner to go into the kitchen on the left. There, in the brightly coloured kitchen, with its cupboards painted turquoise and orange, I'd find a small plate of crisp pale green celery sticks lined with Cheez Whiz that almost matched the orange shade of the cupboards. While I ate the celery, sometimes taking a bite to get the full taste of celery and cheese together or alternately first licking the cheese out of the thin hollows in the celery boat, I told Carol stories about my day in my grade four classroom. She sat with me at the white and gold-flecked arborite kitchen table listening with rapt attention, and in those moments it felt like we were a real mother and daughter.

The downside of Carol not going into work was that she slept in, so she wasn't up in the morning when I left for school. My father left early if Carol wasn't going into the office, and this meant I was on my own in the colourful but quiet kitchen. Preparing and eating breakfast in solitude felt like a lonely way to start the day.

Carol and I had an evening ritual. She came upstairs every night to tuck me into bed and kiss me good night. The white chenille bedspreads had been replaced with matching nylon blue and green bold flowered covers reflecting the "flower power" style that was popular in the late 1960s. Carol sat on the side of my bed, and as she pulled the covers up over my body, we would chat and then the conversation would be punctuated with a final goodnight kiss. I always asked, "Will you be up in the morning?" with an earnestness in my voice, since I preferred having her company at the breakfast table. Usually she replied, "Yes, I will be up," with a cheery and affirming tone. I knew that even if she wasn't going to work the next day, she wanted to make the effort to see me off to school, but sometimes she was just too tired and needed to sleep in.

One evening, midweek, Carol and I were going through our regular bedtime ritual and I asked her the predictable question, "Will you be up in the morning?" Carol looked at me and with a solemn voice responded, "No, I won't be up tomorrow morning." My face must have revealed my disappointment because she drew me close, hugged me very hard, and whispered in my ear, "I love you very much." She was hugging me a little too tight and a little too long, causing me to feel uncomfortable. It didn't feel loving but seemed more like needing. As I squirmed and wiggled away from the embrace, I looked at Carol's face in the dim light for signs of affirmation that everything was all right. Even in the dark I could tell that it wasn't.

I was woken the next morning by both Daddy and Connie, who entered the bedroom together. As I rubbed the sleep from my eyes, I looked over at the bed beside me and noticed that Wendy wasn't there, her bed untouched as if it hadn't been slept in all night. I sat up right away, as it was odd that Connie was home on a weekday morning and that my father was wearing sunglasses at 7:30 a.m.

"What's going on?" I croaked, uttering my first words after a long sleep.

"Something has happened to Carol," said my father in a hollow and distant voice.

Connie stepped forward and sat in the same spot on my bed where Carol had sat the night before.

"We have some bad news. Carol had to go to the hospital," said my sister in a take-charge tone of voice while my dad lingered helplessly in the background, both arms hanging by his side as if he was holding heavy weights.

"She got sick and the ambulance came in the middle of the night."

"What do you mean?" I gasped in disbelief. "Is she okay?"

"No, unfortunately, she didn't make it."

"Didn't make it? Did she die?"

"Yes," Connie calmly responded, touching her hand on my right leg that was still under the covers.

"How could this happen? She was fine last night when she tucked me in."

Shock, disbelief, and fear began to rush over my entire ten-year-old body, but in a moment of utter clarity I asked, "Did she kill herself?"

Chapter 17
Another Death

I DON'T KNOW HOW I KNEW ABOUT THE CONCEPT OF SUICIDE AT ten years old or that it was even possible for someone to choose to end their own life, but Carol's bear-like hug the night before and her expression of love seemed like a goodbye to me.

Connie and Daddy assured me that suicide was not how Carol had died. Apparently, she had ingested some kind of poison when she and my dad had been spraying a wasp nest on the backyard patio a few days before. I recalled seeing Carol and Daddy on their knees on the flagstone patio at dusk spraying a can with a long thin white plastic straw like tube coming out of it. What struck me as odd about that scene was seeing my father and Carol so close together, their bodies touching while they kneeled side by side, their gaze and focus united as one. I had rarely seen any signs of physical affection between them and this closeness stood out in stark contrast to my sense of them as a couple.

"Why didn't you get sick from the poison, Daddy?" I questioned my father while my brain tried to process Carol's sudden illness and death.

"I don't know. I think Carol must have inhaled more of the fumes than I did."

At the time I didn't understand that at age thirty-four, Carol was young to have such an untimely and tragic death. I had lumped all adults into one group as "old" and in my world, death had already happened so the logic of adults getting sick and dying fit into my belief system.

It wasn't until I was twenty-two years old that I learned that Carol had killed herself. I was at Connie's house for dinner and I don't remember how the topic of Carol came up in our conversation, but Connie referred to the time when Carol "committed suicide." "What? Carol committed suicide?" I gasped. People still used the term *committed* then, as if taking your own life was a criminal act, like murder. "Yes, she took sleeping pills, in the middle of the night. You must remember that, don't you?" Connie said in a calm and casual tone, like we were reminiscing about some typical milestone of our family life.

I had believed the story about Carol dying from the poison that she and Daddy had sprayed on the wasp nest, right up until this moment. I explained this to Connie while my mind tried to process so many conflicting feelings at once: shock, sadness, betrayal, anger, and wisdom. "I remember asking if Carol had killed herself the morning after it happened and, Connie, you said no, she didn't kill herself.

"Well, you were so young, I couldn't believe it, but you did ask right away if she had taken her own life. Daddy and I thought it best to protect you from knowing this awful truth."

Which was worse? The awful truth or a lie to protect me? What if my suspicions at the time had been validated? Would it have made a difference? The familiar feeling of loneliness I had as the youngest in my family, kept in the dark about so many things, re-emerged, awakening my profound loss and grief.

Carol's funeral was at Temple Emanuel, a reform Jewish temple on Old Colony Road in North York. The temple was old only in its street name. It was built in the early 1960s and my mother and father were part of the growing number of Jews in the suburbs in the 1950s who helped to found this place of worship. Rabbi Arthur Bielfeld, a young pale white-skinned man in his early thirties with a mass of short tight brown curls, presided over the funeral service. While I think my father played a role in the hiring of Rabbi Bielfeld, it was clear that he didn't like or respect him much. He called him a *fagola*, which was a derogatory Yiddish word for a gay man. I didn't understand the meaning of the word at the time, but my father was reprimanded by my sisters every time he used it, which was frequently.

Since Carol had converted to Judaism, her funeral was to be held in Temple Emanuel, even though she had spent most of her life as a Christian. Aunt Phil, Uncle Bill, Harold, Lillian, and David attended the small gathering, likely feeling out of place with the Jewish rituals of death, the mourners kaddish being recited: "Yis-gaddal, v'yis-kadash…." These are the only words I remember and when I say them out loud now, they conjure up memories of so many losses in my family, both Mommy and Carol and the many more yet to come.

It was a solemn and quiet service, and I was struck at seeing adults lose control and cry. I was instructed not to talk about how Carol had died because this might upset people. I didn't question the authority of the adults in my world and acquiesced to this request.

While Jews have closed caskets and are not buried in street clothes, Carol's family wanted her buried in the outfit she had worn at her wedding when she and my father had left for their honeymoon. A vibrant blue and green-flecked wool suit with matching pencil skirt and jacket was retrieved out of its plastic dry-cleaning cover and given to the funeral home for Carol to be dressed in. I don't know if my father did this to appease her family and if she was actually buried wearing this outfit, but I was glad to see it again. I loved this suit and I remember how put-together and beautiful Carol looked in it. I was especially drawn to the blue and green and I found comfort in the warm, soft texture. My Barbie doll had a ballgown in these same colours, and it was my most favourite and treasured outfit. The gown had a fitted, shiny green-satin sheath that slipped over Barbie's incredibly thin and buxom body, with blue pieces of tulle all around her slim waist, creating a lacy and floating look.

I touched the fabric of Carol's suit one more time before it was taken away and I was overcome with an ache of all that I was losing.

Chapter 18
The Gruesome Threesome

PHILLIP STEWART CALLED US THE GRUESOME THREESOME. HE WAS the much older brother of my friend Valerie, a man really, who often made fun of Valerie, Susan Stinson, and I because we always hung out together. Valerie snapped insults at Phillip whenever he said, "Oh here comes the gruesome threesome" with a self-satisfied smirk. I wasn't sure why this made her so upset. I was glad we had "grew some" and didn't understand the nuance of the word until much later.

We were definitely a threesome and spent hours playing together at the Stewarts' house in the valley – down the street from 77 Plymbridge – because it had two fascinating and private places where we were free to do whatever we pleased. While Valerie's parents, Phillip, and her other three siblings, Mark, Wayne, and Becky, were always home, there was a lack of supervision that allowed us to play with wild abandon.

We spent time in the dark and spooky basement uncovering the Ouija board to find answers to our life dilemmas. Susan, with her perfectly combed, silky shoulder-length red hair (she said she brushed it one hundred times per night) and milky white skin, always wanted to know which boy loved her. The possibilities for her seemed endless because each week a different boy's name was spelled out, with the triangular planchette of the Ouija moving swiftly and confidently across the board. Valerie and I had more pressing life questions to ponder, since neither of our lives were as picture-perfect as Susan's.

While Valerie's family was intact, the house she lived in was not. Their large beautiful stone home, set back on a well-manicured garden on the outside, did not reveal what was happening on the inside. Clutter and chaos filled every room, getting progressively worse when you descended from the second floor to the basement. I didn't know that homes could be messy and dirty like the Stewarts. Dishes left unwashed in the sink in the narrow galley kitchen, magazines and newspapers stacked unread in piles, and plates with old uneaten food littered every room like a trail left by a raccoon who had picked through the trash on garbage night.

The lure of the Ouija board in the basement was what got me down there since the stench of mould and mildew at the top of the narrow wooden stairs was a serious deterrent, not to mention the piles of boxes oozing clothes, tools, books and other mysterious items that had to be manoeuvred around to get to our clearing on the cold damp floor where we sat to find out our fortunes. After several minutes my nose adjusted, and I was immersed in the magic of the Ouija and the secrets we shared.

The other private spot at Valerie's was behind her house down by the Don River, where it smelled of pine needles, cedar trees, and the fresh outdoors. Valerie's father had built a six-foot by eight-foot wood cabin by the river, where we spent endless summer days and nights creating a world of fantasy, fun, and adventure. With a real wooden door that closed and a cutout open window facing the river, we all pretended that this was where we really lived. We took on various roles in our "household," with Valerie being the adventurer who went off to sea, sailing on the thick rope swing that went clear across the river if you took a running leap for the rope. Susan seemed happily stuck in the role of homemaker, often sweeping out the cabin with a straw broom, telling us we couldn't go in until she was done. I fell somewhere in between, not being brave enough to venture onto the rope swing (I still hadn't learned to swim) and rejecting the domesticity that Susan had chosen. This allowed both of them to give me tasks to complete to add depth and detail to the characters they had carved out. One such task was to find an object that could be used for a potty. Not wanting to venture out of our fantasy land to attend to the reality of bodily functions, I found an old chipped white enamel pot that we put in the cabin to use when needed. When the cabin started to develop an earthy acrid smell of urine, we moved the toilet outdoors and stood guard for each other when we needed to use it. The cabin was a magical oasis in the woods that provided us all with an unchecked freedom in nature. With no sense of time, we stayed at the cabin in the spring, summer, and fall evenings until we heard an adult yell somewhere in the distance, "Time to come home, it's getting dark."

Back we went then to our homes, which were only a short walk away. Susan, to her perfect family with four kids and a mom and dad in her sprawling split-level white brick home with the backyard pool, and Valerie back inside to her unkempt house. I knew there must be more than just disarray in Valerie's home since her appearance portrayed something amiss as well. Valerie looked the opposite of Susan. Her skin was not creamy like Susan's, more like skim milk with a bluish tint that accentuated the dark circles under her eyes. With her messy tangled brown hair and rumpled clothes, Valerie looked more like a motherless child than I did.

Chapter 19
Getting around Hoggs Hollow

TO LIVE IN HOGGS HOLLOW, OR WHAT WE CALLED "THE VALLEY," WAS to live in a community where almost everybody knew you. There were two sides to the valley, separated by the Don River in between. A short, paved bridge allowed one car at a time to cross the river to the other side. There was a grassy hill at the wing wall, just where the bridge started, that you could climb down and then sit on the concrete footings at the bottom. It was nicely hidden and provided a future spot for Valerie, Susan, and I to take up smoking cigarettes in our adolescence. A huge old millstone from the last mill in the valley, the Pratt mill, sat on a pedestal at the other end of the bridge. The millstone platform was placed at the tip of a small triangular piece of grass and had an open cedar rail fence all around it. It was a perfect meeting spot – "Meet you at the millstone" was the phrase we all used. We rarely went to the other side of the valley but knew people who lived there: the Creeds, the Kofflers, and the Lepofskys, all of whom created legacies in Toronto – Creed Furs, Shoppers Drug Mart, and David Lepofosky, who was my age, visually impaired, and became an ardent activist for the blind. He was the one who implemented the practice of TTC drivers calling out all bus and subway stops to improve accessibility.

When I walked down the street on our side of the valley with my friends, we knew the name of every person who drove by. Often they'd stop and ask if we wanted a ride, as it was a long walk in from the outside world, York Mills and Yonge Street, or our public school. "Uncle" Weary always picked up any child who was walking in the valley. He wasn't really our uncle, but that's what we called him. An older man with an abundance of thick white hair, bright blue eyes and a big bulbous red nose, he lived across the street from my good friend Leigh Harris. He and his wife had no children and lived in a little white house that resembled a cottage. It was set back from the road down a long thin gravel laneway. It didn't matter how many of us there were or where we were going, Uncle Weary always stopped his big white car and all of us climbed in. His blue eyes twinkled with glee and he turned around and talked to us in the back seat in his animated wheezy voice that sounded a bit like he had marbles in his mouth.

"Where are you going, kids?" The question was rhetorical since he often just took us for a drive even if we were right in front of our own homes. Our answer was always the same. "Drive crazy, Uncle Weary, drive crazy!" we all yelled in unison. He acted as if he didn't know what we meant and start driving along slowly and then suddenly we were headed straight for a tree or a house and he veered away at the last minute. We squealed with both fear and delight, buckling over with laughter secure in the fact that never in all these drives had he every really crashed. Uncle Weary acted all surprised after the simulated crash and he'd turn around and talk to us in the back seat while he drove. "What? What happened?"

"Do it again, Uncle Weary, do it again. Drive crazy!" we shouted.

I guess someone's parents found out about our joy rides because one day Uncle Weary drove right past us on our way home from school and we all yelled and ran to chase his car down for a ride. He stopped the car, rolled down his big square window, and said, "Not today, kids." We pleaded with him, hanging off the window, and his usual mischievous eyes were downcast when he said he'd been told not to pick us up anymore. I don't know who had told on him, but when I lamented to my father about missing Uncle Weary's car rides, he frowned, pulled his thick dark black brows together, and yelled, "You are not to get in the car with that man, do you hear me? What the hell is an old drunk man doing driving kids around in his car like that anyways?"

I felt sorry for Uncle Weary because he didn't have any kids and I knew how much he enjoyed being with us. He was the only other adult I knew, other than Daddy, who was so fun and playful.

One day, when Leigh, Susan, Valerie, and I were making our thirty-minute walk to school, we approached the house that belonged to the judge. We didn't know his name but just knew that a magistrate lived in the house that was tucked behind the hedges. As we walked past his house, the door of a parked black limousine opened and we were asked by the judge, who was sitting in the back seat, if we wanted a ride to school. Our mouths opened wide in disbelief. We looked back and forth at one another, trying to register if this was okay. He assured us that he was passing right by our school and he was glad to have the company. We all climbed in, as the driver with his black suit, tie, and matching black hat with a plastic rim (like the milkman) held the door for four ten-year-olds. Nobody talked and it was a quiet smooth ride in the five minutes it took to get to school.

From then on, we synchronized our walk to school to reach the judge's house at the exact time we had been picked up, slowing down our pace if we didn't see the limo or speeding up if it was parked there. It wasn't consistent, but we did receive a few more rides with him. We felt grown-up and important when chauffeured to school in his sleek black vehicle. It was a stark contrast to our wild and adventurous rides with Uncle Weary in his crazy white car. The two experiences exposed me to men who were different from my father: taken seriously by one, yet indulged in a playfulness with the other.

In the valley everyone knew one another and the adults looked out for all the children. It was a time of innocence and trust. Nobody locked their front doors. We always felt safe. To live in the valley was to live in a community. The cliché "It takes a village" was not a phrase we knew then, yet it was exactly the life I grew up with in our little enclave.

Chapter 20
Friends in the Valley

THE GROSHIPS WERE OUR NEIGHBOURS ON ONE SIDE OF OUR HOUSE and the McAlpines were on the other side. I never knew any adults' first names. We always called all adults by their last names: Mr. and Mrs. Groship and Mrs. McAlpine. The two families were starkly different in both physical appearance and in the style of their homes.

Mrs. McAlpine's husband had died and she lived alone, but her grown son visited often. She was overweight, with puffy red cheeks and ear-length white hair that curled in ringlets at the ends and was combed back at the front to reveal a receding hairline. Mrs. McAlpine always wore suits with skirts that swished when she walked. Her low-heeled pumps displayed small mounds of flesh that puffed out of her shoes, as if the toes and heels fit but the rest of her foot couldn't be contained. Her dog, McDuff, not only matched her in the prefix of their names, but also in race and ethnicity, being a white Scottish terrier. They also walked the same, slowly waddling from side to side when they sauntered in the yard, with McDuff following his mistress wherever she went.

Her house had dark wood furniture with a formal dining room that had floral chintz-covered chairs and a hutch crammed with crystal ware and fancy dishes.

My father said Mrs. McAlpine was anti-Semitic. I didn't know what this meant, but it sounded a lot like *antiseptic*, which did fit with her clean, spotless house. She would be upset if the leaves from our tree blew into her backyard. She took pride in her garden and had a colourful array of flowers in both the front and back of her house. While Mrs. McAlpine liked me and called me "dear," it was evident she was not a fan of my father. She never greeted him when they were both outside and there were no invitations for him to come and visit. I don't know what Daddy did —or didn't do —to deserve her rejection, but perhaps she felt the mere presence of this dark-skinned, unmarried Jewish man sullied the neighbourhood.

The Groships were an older couple also, and their house was modern with stark white furniture that was all angled and curved. They had what my dad called "abstract art" on the wall. He claimed that he could throw some black paint on a white canvas, call it *Black on White*, and then, "I could sell it for thousands of dollars as modern art and none of those cockamamie critics would know the difference."

The Groships didn't have any children, at least not human ones. They had chihuahuas, seven of them: Princess, Precious, Peony, Prince, Priscilla, Pearl, and Picasso. Mrs. Groship talked to their dogs so lovingly in that high-pitched voice that mothers often use with their babies – "Motherese," they call it now.

"How is my sweet Precious? Come and sit on Mamma's lap. Now, Prince, don't be jealous, you can sit on Mamma's lap too."

I could hear the Groships talking to their dogs since our backyard patios were adjacent to one another. A large green cedar hedge blocked visibility but not sound. My father took advantage of this living wall of privacy and often, when all seven of the chihuahuas were "yelping," as he called it, he put the hose through the cedar border and sprayed them all to "shut them up." It worked immediately and one by one they whimpered and ran away. I always felt sorry for the little dogs when he did this and also worried that the Groships would step onto their patio and witness my father committing this crime. We had a good relationship with the Groships and I didn't want him to ruin this.

The Groships often had us over for a delicious dinner prepared by their live-in cook, Harry. It seemed odd that they had a male chef who cooked just for them. Harry was the first Chinese person I ever met and while his real name was not Harry, we were told that was the name he preferred. Harry was an older man who spoke very little English and he was always wearing a white chef's jacket. He nodded his head up and down when you talked to him and smiled, showing his many missing teeth.

Harry cooked gourmet meals every night in the gleaming white kitchen. Sometimes I sat perched on one of the turquoise stools that faced the counter and watched him chop and dice vegetables using a big square-bladed knife. The Groships said Harry made regional Chinese food. I didn't know what that meant, but it sure tasted different than the food we ordered from Sea-Hi and Moonglow.

All my friends lived in the valley and we went to the same elementary school, York Mills Public School. Valerie, Susan, and Leigh were my everyday friends. Glorianne Naiman was my Jewish family friend. She had two sisters, Sandy and Elaine, who were both the same age as my sisters, Connie and Wendy. Her parents, Arnie and Annette, were also friends with my parents, so when we were all together – when my mom was alive – there was a friend for everyone. The Naimans also had a yacht that they kept at Lake Simcoe. We went on several family boating vacations with them, visiting the Thirty Thousand Islands in Georgian Bay as well as the Thousand Islands near Kingston. Both my dad and Arnie were short men – five feet, six inches – and they always seemed to have a competition going on between them. My dad bought his boat, *Beverley III*, which was thirty-two feet long, and then Mr. Naiman bought a boat that was just a little bigger at thirty-six feet. To them, size did matter.

Annette and my mom shared recipes. When I look in the 1950 edition of *Naomi Jewish Women's Cookbook* that belonged to my mother, at the back of the weathered blue cloth book I see a recipe for Asian Sesame Chicken in my mother's handwriting, with Annette

Naiman's name written in the top right-hand corner of the page, acknowledging the recipe's origins.

Shelley Gibb lived in a small house down the street and she only had a mother. She said her parents fought all the time and her dad had moved out. Shelley's mom worked full-time, which was unusual then because most of the mothers in the valley were full-time homemakers. Shelley was often alone after school and I hung out with her, feeling a sense of comradery that there were other families who could be different and have only one parent like me.

Christine McCartney was on the corner at the end of Plymbridge and she was for fun and adventure, Kooky Christine. She could, on command, breathe in through her nose and make her two nostrils stick together for a record amount of time. Her face turned red, but she kept going.

I also had male friends in the valley. Loudie Owen, who lived directly across from us beside the large, steep tree-lined hill that we called the ravine. We often took a short cut home from school and ended up right beside Loudie's house. If his father, Selwyn, saw us coming down the ravine, he would yell at us: "Get off my property!" Since the hill extended for more than fifty metres in diameter and was all trees, I didn't see how he "owned" this property, so we usually ignored his bark and continued on our way. As quiet and soft-spoken as Loudie was, his father was the opposite. Somehow their names were mixed up or maybe Loudie's dad was hoping for someone brash like himself, but Loudie never did grow into his name.

Loudie's family came from England. Once, his mother, Violet, went on a trip home to England and came back with a housekeeper named Daisy. Daisy seemed to do more than just keep the house clean. She also kept company with Violet. Violet and Daisy had tea together, shopped together, went to movies, and often travelled together, without Selwyn. One day a For Sale sign appeared on Loudie's front lawn. He said that he was moving away with his dad and brother because his mom and Daisy had gone off to England to live together.

All the neighbours gossiped about how the "lady" of the house and the housekeeper could possibly be friends. I learned later that there was a name for when two women loved each other, but what seemed odd to me at the time was the class difference.

David Berman was my other male friend. He had an older sister, Evie, short for Evelyn, who was friends with my sister Connie. The Bermans were also Jewish and seemed to live large. They had a big swimming pool with a sign that read, "We don't swim in your toilet, so don't pee in our pool," which did make perfect sense so I followed the rule. Their pool was encased in stone on the outside and it faced the front of the street, which was odd. Most people had a pool in their backyard, but they didn't have a backyard, just a ravine. They had not one but two kitchens: one upstairs and one downstairs, to keep kosher. Mrs. Berman was always cooking up a storm and nourished me when I came over to play with David. She pinched my cheek and fed me delicious roast chicken, telling me to "Eat, eat!" watching with pleasure as I savoured each delicious bite.

Mrs. Harris, Leigh's mom, baked us our daily chocolate cake. At the end of the school day we walked right in through the unlocked front door and headed to the kitchen. There, sitting on the counter, was a covered silver platter. We lifted the lid to find a warm freshly baked chocolate cake. Sitting at the kitchen table eating a large piece of luscious, moist homemade layered cake with thick chocolate icing, accompanied by a cold glass of milk to wash it all down, was a slice of heaven.

Every day in summer, when I wasn't at camp, I hung out at the Stinsons. They lived one door away from the Bermans. With a pool in the backyard and four children, their house was a hub for all the kids in the neighbourhood. Mrs. Stinson welcomed everyone and always fed us tasty snacks in the backyard by the pool: Rice Krispie squares, potato chips, and freezies. When tall, blond Mr. Stinson came home swinging his briefcase up the path, we all dispersed to go to our own homes for dinner. Mrs. Stinson called me "Mush." I don't know why she called me that, but I loved this term of endearment that she had just for me. She was my go-to mother, and whenever something happened to me, she was there. Once, I was running home from school and fell on the hard pavement and chipped my tooth. There was blood everywhere. I went crying to the Stinsons, and sure enough Mrs. Stinson took me to the hospital to have it looked after. She knew my dad was at work and just filled in the gaps.

I didn't swim in the pool with the other kids, so she spent a part of every day with me alone in the pool and we picked up where I left off at camp, blowing bubbles. Without saying anything about it, she gradually helped me to feel comfortable in the water and by the end of the summer I had learned how to swim. I loved Mrs. Stinson. Part of me just wanted to move into their house where there wasn't a chance of ever being alone.

I was rich with food and friends growing up in the valley. The community embraced me and I was provided with many opportunities for kinship and connection with endearing and quirky characters. This carried me through my youth.

Chapter 21
Henry

AFTER CAROL DIED, WE HAD A STEADY STREAM OF HOUSEKEEPERS come and go. Since the live-in experience with Helen and the Strains didn't go too well, my father thought it best to hire someone who could come and go on a daily basis to be there for me when I came home from school, as well as to clean, do laundry, and prepare dinner. They could then leave by 6:00 or 6:30 p.m., when Daddy came home from work. The only memorable thing about all these women was the consistent meals they prepared. Consistently bad. To be efficient, meals were prepared in the afternoon and then kept warm in the oven until my father came home. It seemed we were always eating a dried-up piece of meat (after two hours in the oven, it was hard to tell what it was), a few shrivelled once-frozen vegetables, and watery potatoes. Wendy and I made jokes and laughed hysterically about the dinners: "Wonder what we're having for dinner tonight? Mystery meat and peas, what a nice change." My father never complained or laughed, but ate silently, unable to speak while he chewed away on a piece of meat like a dog with a rawhide bone.

Since the Groships had a male cook, my father, ahead of his time in wanting to be an equal-opportunity employer, hired Henry, a male, to be our housekeeper/cleaner. Henry didn't cook but came highly recommended from one of Daddy's friends as an excellent cleaner. My dad thought he could manage the meals himself by stocking up on Swanson frozen TV dinners. This was fine with me. I loved the aluminum tray with little compartments that separated each food group from one another. My favourite meal was the chicken dinner. The breaded chicken took up most of the real estate in the hexagonal space at the front of the tray, with corn on one side and creamy mashed potatoes on the other, both flanking the main course. The apple cobbler dessert separated the vegetables, right in the middle. The dessert had a cellophane cover that was to be kept on until after you finished the main course. I snuck bites of the warm gooey apple as I ate, delighting in the fact that dessert could be eaten throughout the meal. Since most of the food was the same colour, my dad couldn't distinguish which pale creamy blob was on my fork.

Henry only came once a week to clean and it was hard to tell what day of the week that was. The only evidence that he had been there was the missing envelope that was left for him on the kitchen table with his pay. The house didn't seem a whole lot cleaner. Henry's appearance didn't seem to fit the image of what someone who cleans for a living should look like. A middle-aged man with uncombed grey hair, thick black-rimmed glasses, and a large belly that protruded out over his baggy trousers, he often looked a little rumpled and unkempt, like he'd just rolled out of bed after a restless night sleeping in his clothes.

There was something about Henry that made me feel uncomfortable, yet I couldn't quite name what it was. I told Daddy, "Henry is creepy" but he just said, "You're not used to a male cleaner and you should give him a chance."

One day I came home early from school to find Henry's car in the driveway. Henry and I rarely crossed paths because he was usually gone before I came home from school. I walked in the front door with some trepidation, my gut flip-flopping like a fish out of water. "Hi, Henry," I called out in an attempt to be friendly while I shut the door. No answer. "Henry?" I projected my voice a little louder. Still no answer. The house was lifeless and quiet, no evidence of cleansers or a vacuum anywhere. I walked around looking in every room, calling out his name. No visible sign of Henry. I walked through the kitchen toward the basement door and saw the door ajar and a light on at the bottom of the basement stairs. After the Strains had left, we turned the basement into a sitting room with comfy chairs and made use of the little bar area that had a sink and fridge by adding three stools that lined up against the bar counter. While I slowly descended the stairs, I could see Henry sitting very still in one of the big overstuffed chairs, his eyes vacant and expressionless, as if his body was present but the rest of him had got up and left the room. "Henry? What are you doing?" I asked. "I am cleaning," he muttered, as if exhausted from his work. Having been all over the house, I could see no evidence of his labour. I walked toward Henry while he sat motionless in the chair and at last had proof of what he had been cleaning. It was 80% proof Canadian Club Whiskey. On the floor beside Henry was a half-empty 26-ounce bottle. My father, who was not a drinker, received many bottles of Canadian Club at Christmas each year from his clients and he kept these stored in the basement bar. Other than offering guests a drink from time to time, these bottles largely remained untouched. Henry had done a pretty good job of cleaning out the bar. "Please don't tell your father," he mumbled in a monotone voice, spittle from his mouth escaping as he talked. "I cleaned all day and I just needed a rest." Not knowing what to do, Henry's inebriated statement motivated me to call my father right away at his office.

That was the end of Henry. My father gave him one more envelope and then threw away all the whiskey bottles that had been filled with tap water. Daddy's track record in hiring reliable domestic help was becoming quite dismal. Absent from home due to his demanding work schedule as the head of his own chartered accountant company, and lacking the ability to address issues with the household help, my father took refuge with the one group of mammals he thought he could train and control: dogs.

Chapter 22
"Kennel Up"

AS AN OUTSIDER, IF YOU WERE LISTENING TO OUR FAMILY CONVERsations, you wouldn't know if we were talking about the dog or the housekeeper because all our pets had human names: Barney, Andy, Cindy, Tina, and Tracy. We always had a pet dog in our home. Unlike the hired help, the dogs were trained. Each dog that came to live with us had to attend the obligatory obedience school. My father exerted his power and control and was the master of every canine that entered his domain. Each dog went off to boarding school for several weeks to learn to obey the master and be trained for hunting. Daddy liked to go to northern Ontario and hunt for ducks, pheasant, geese, moose, and deer. The dogs we had were usually retrievers who were trained to bring back the kill. After the dog came back from training, they were introduced to their new home, the kennel.

No dog ever slept inside the house. Daddy thought that would pamper them. The pet could hang out in the house during the day, but at bedtime my father issued the command "Kennel up" and the dog immediately went to the back door, waiting to be put in the kennel; tail wagging, wet nose pointed at the door, listening expectantly for my father's predictable steps and the door to be opened.

The kennel was a long, narrow, rectangular twenty-five-foot by three-foot concrete run surrounded by a metal chain-link fence on both sides as well as on the roof. It was built at the perimeter of our backyard abutting the Don River. Every other day, the concrete floor of the kennel was hosed down so all the dog's excrement could be washed into the Don River. I remember using the jet sprayer on the hose and aiming it at the human-like turds that were collected in little piles, trying to get enough force behind each pile to push it through the chain-link fence and roll down the hill. There was no consciousness then about the environment. No one I knew thought about those things. People threw trash out the window of their cars, the word *recycling* wasn't even part of our lexicon. I think our dogs' waste likely contributed to the pollution of the Don River.

My father had a fire-engine red hydrant placed midway in the kennel so that the male dogs could pee on it. I don't know where or how he got this hydrant that was clearly meant for residential areas, but it was always a conversation piece when guests and neighbours came to visit. The dogs, however, never used it.

At the end of the kennel was a thirty-inch by thirty-two-inch doghouse. Constructed of particle board and painted dark green, the doghouse had a slanted roof and a square opening where the dog could enter and exit. Inside this fairly crude structure was a scattering of straw and a heat lamp to keep the dog warm during the cold winter nights.

While our family pets did obey my father and saw him as the master, they all rebelled against him in their own unique way, demonstrating their independence.

Barney was a stocky golden Labrador who was hyperactive. He didn't make it through training school. The trainer called one day and said Barney had jumped up and bit his lip. The trainer had never seen this before in all his years of training dogs. My father had Barney put down because, he said, "The dog can't be trusted to be around children." I was glad I had escaped any calamity.

Daddy believed he had taught Andy, a shiny black lab with an energetic and engaging personality, how to smile. When guests came over, he demonstrated this feat by saying, "Smile, Andy, smile," and then he would hold his cigar up to Andy's face. Even I could tell as a child that the dog was only grimacing from the cigar smoke. Andy chose when he performed or did not, often frustrating my father. Guests would tire of my dad's repetitive command, recognizing that it wouldn't induce any living thing to smile.

Cindy, a golden lab, kept escaping from my father's regimen and regularly ran away from home. We were frequently outside the front door, with the door ajar, yelling in the street over and over again, calling for Cindy at the top of our lungs. Cindy wanted freedom. Poor Cindy paid a price for her freedom; in the end, she got hit by a car.

Tina and Tracey were two German shorthaired pointers that were sisters. My father had the idea that they could keep each other company. Tina was a gentle, loving obedient dog, while her sibling was as wild as they come. Tracy spent hours running up and down the dozen stairs that led from the first floor to the second in our house.

Daddy put a collapsible wooden baby gate at the foot of the stairs as a deterrent, but Tracy just jumped right over it and ran up and down, up and down, in an oscillating repetitive rhythm, like a yo-yo. I invited Valerie and Susan over and we encouraged (she didn't need much convincing) Tracy to run up and down the stairs. Once she started, she never stopped, only circling around to manoeuvre her change of direction at both the top and bottom of the staircase.

My father sent Tracy and her obsessive-compulsive disorder to a farm. He said she needed to run free. I could see the logic in that.

Tina was the one dog that lived with us for many years, until I was nineteen, and she provided a predictable and calming presence. I was yearning for a woman or mother figure who could come and do this for us as well. Just when I was about to give up hope, Mrs. Williams entered our lives.

Chapter 23
Mrs. Williams

MRS. WILLIAMS DIDN'T LIVE IN AT THE BEGINNING BUT CAME EVERY weekday, leaving three dried-up pork chops and some peas in the oven behind her each afternoon for Daddy, Wendy, and me to eat for our dinner at 6:30 p.m.

She was called by her last name – I never knew her first name – as she commanded respect. A tall, large black woman with puffed-up, rounded cheeks and eyes that radiated joy behind her light-coloured cat-eye glasses, she was my Mary Poppins.

Mrs. Williams was a slow-moving, slow-speaking woman who made all the mundane details of housekeeping and what we now call "self-care" come alive for me. I came home from school to the smell of starch and freshly ironed shirts in the kitchen. I didn't remember seeing anyone iron before and it intrigued me to see how Mrs. Williams had set up shop in our kitchen, with the plastic laundry basket piled with clean clothes right on top of the kitchen table, an ironing board adjacent to the table bearing a sizzling, steaming-hot iron. The pressed clothes were hung up around the kitchen like we were Parkers Cleaners, where my father took all his shirts before Mrs. Williams came along. It wasn't only shirts that she ironed, but sheets and underwear too – all the wrinkled, crumpled clean laundry in that basket was pressed until smooth and stiff like a soldier in uniform.

While folding laundry, Mrs. Williams made keen observations about the daily habits of my father, which shocked and titillated me.

"Oh, Mr. Barrett's pyjama bottoms are wearing thin, him has been rubbing his balls," she drawled in her Jamaican patois dialect.

I laughed, red with embarrassment as at eleven years old I was just becoming curious and interested in boys and their anatomy. Mrs. Williams said this in such a matter-of-fact way, holding up evidence of my dad's pyjama bottoms that were threadbare in the crotch. I accepted it as truth.

She shuffled around the house in what were once fuzzy, but now well-worn, size-twelve mule slippers. Even though she walked at a snail's pace, she invariably lost a slipper in her stroll and then she would stop in her tracks, let out a big sigh, and say, "Me has lost my slipper," reversing slowly to step back into the lost footwear. I loved this mishap in her step and learned to imitate it to perfection, copying her voice, inflection, and movement. Wendy and her friends often asked for my impersonation of Mrs. Williams and I imitated the lost slipper scene repeatedly to peals of laughter.

Watching Mrs. Williams's ritual of applying lotion to her face and hands at the end of the day is a memory for me of sight, sound, smell, and sensation. There was beauty and comfort in how she poured the lotion, smoothed it slowly into her black velvet skin, saying, "Ah, I need to cream my skin so." When Mrs. Williams left in the late afternoon, the spot where she had sat smelled of a lemony freshness.

The daily commute back and forth to our house was wearing on Mrs. Williams, especially the walk in and out of the valley. At her pace, the travelling time was likely doubled. I was overjoyed when my father asked her to live in and stay in our basement and she accepted. We cleaned out the basement and Mrs. Williams moved in, bringing her dark wood and upholstered furniture with her. I was told not to bother her at the end of the day or go downstairs when she was off work because she shouldn't be disturbed. I respected this boundary and at long last felt a sense of security, calm, and nurturing in our household. I loved Mrs. Williams and could talk to her about school, my friends, and boys. She seemed to have wisdom and delivered her advice in one-line proverbs: "Wise monkey know what tree to climb." She was never in a rush, was always home, and had time for me.

We settled into a routine and dinners improved when my father encouraged her to cook food using her own recipes. We then enjoyed chicken rich with spicy sauce, rice and peas, and bananas she called plantain, which she fried in oil, creating a sweet, rich smell in the kitchen. On weekends, she often stayed with her son, Adrian, and his wife.

Mrs. Williams stayed with us for two years and in that time I began to discover that boys could be more than friends. Wendy, who was eighteen, had discovered boys long ago and was adventurous, experimenting with a wide variety of them. While their names were different, she was drawn to the same type: risk-takers, who lived life on the edge. Connie was the opposite. She dated a few Jewish boys, but was going steady with one, Saul. He gave her a gold pin that came from the university he went to. She was proud of this pin, which had a small suspended gold chain, and attached it to all her clothing and went around saying she was "pinned." I didn't know what this meant but thought that the jewellery was lacking in sparkle. My father was also dating and there was one woman who came over quite often. Her name was Brenda and, like Carol, she was my dad's secretary.

It was good that Mrs. Williams wasn't there on the weekends, to see all the comings and goings. While she didn't have a husband, nor ever spoke of ever having one, it was clear she had opinions about people. "Show me your company, tells me who you are."

Eventually, Mrs. Williams had to leave. Her son, Adrian, had a new baby and he asked her to come and live with him and his wife to help raise their child. This chubby, adorable baby boy had usurped me. I was sad and jealous and realized my otherness: a twelve-year-old motherless girl. Mrs. Williams's connection to me was not real family, but employment after all. She had, however, been a nurturing mother to me and what I learned from her was joy, comfort, laughter, and not to rush the daily rituals of life. There is beauty in the simple act of creaming one's skin.

Chapter 24
Piano Lessons

DADDY THOUGHT I SHOULD BE A PIANIST. I DIDN'T REALLY HAVE any interest in playing the piano, but he said it would be good to learn to play an instrument, a potential career path for me. Both Connie and Wendy had taken skating lessons when they were young, but I had never done any after-school activities, except Brownies.

I was signed up for piano lessons at York Mills Public School when I was eight years old. A piano teacher named Mrs. Fowler taught group lessons after school in the gym every Tuesday. A small group – eight of us – took turns practising on the old upright wooden piano that sat in the corner. Mrs. Fowler gave each of us a foldout cardboard keyboard that was an exact replica of the piano keys, to practise our finger formation and learn what the notes were. We were to practise each week at home. We didn't have a piano. I asked Daddy, "How am I supposed to practise and learn how to play piano if we don't have one?"

"Practise on your cardboard keyboard," he said. This made no sense at all to me.

Mrs. Fowler reinforced my theory of how names and personality went together like bread and butter. An older woman with grey hair that flipped under in big thick curls just below her ears, she often wore a foul expression. We all were scared of her because she could get angry and snap at us at any moment, if we hadn't done our homework or practised. One day, it was my turn to go to the piano to play a scale and I was making a lot of mistakes. "Marsha, did you practise these scales at home last week on the piano?" she barked, causing the other kids to look up from their two-dimensional keyboards in dread. How could I tell her that I didn't have a piano?

Not knowing what to say, my mouth dry with fear, I simply eked out "No" in a timid voice.

Mrs. Fowler jolted back the piano bench we were sitting on, making a loud screeching noise on the shiny gym floor. She stood up and tore the sheet music off the stand, throwing it onto the ground. She started hurling all kinds of stuff around the room: music books, pencils, and some kids' cardboard keyboards, screaming, "How can I teach any of you when you don't practise?" The room was silent while we all looked down at the floor in panic, stealing sideways glances at one another, not sure what to say or do. With her curls askew, Mrs. Fowler then started picking up all the things she had flung around the room, jamming them into her big black briefcase that looked like a doctor's bag. She headed for the exit, pushed one of the big silver bars on the double doors, and left.

We huddled together in shock, fear, and relief. Nobody thought about going to the office or telling any adults. We just packed up our fake keyboards and headed home early.

"How was piano today?" Daddy asked over dinner that night. I told him about Mrs. Fowler's fit and that I was too scared to go back to that class. He agreed, saying that that kind of behaviour was inappropriate and he would be meeting with the school principal, Mr. Chambers, to let him have a "piece of his mind." I asked why I was taking lessons at all, since we didn't even own a piano. I wasn't going to go far on a cardboard keyboard.

Daddy bought a piano. I went from having a paper keyboard that made no noise to one that played all by itself.

He bought what was called a player piano. It was a modern upright piano made of light brown wood, modelled after the old-fashioned player pianos from the late nineteenth and early twentieth centuries.

The music the piano played was on perforated paper tubes that you fit between two notches. These tubes rolled, once you pushed the little black button on the console on the left-hand side of the piano. It was magical to see the white and black keys move all by themselves, producing beautiful melodies. Daddy bought a selection of music rolls, show tunes being his favourite. Each roll came in its own narrow brown cardboard box. I was told to be very careful when lifting these out because if you made any tears or rips, the music wouldn't play.

Daddy never tired of sitting down at the piano when unsuspecting guests came over, to demonstrate his new piano-playing skills. He'd secretly push the button, sit down, and coordinate his fingers to follow along with the self-moving keys. Then, at a well-timed moment, he would lift his hands while the ivory bars continued to move on their own, carrying the tune. The reaction was always the same: mouths open in surprise and then peals of laughter. You could even press buttons for a honky-tonk sound, which he especially loved to do on the song "Those Were the Days." That was one of his favourite songs to play, or perhaps the other rolls were torn, since we had a steady repetitive stream of "Those were the days, my friend, we thought they'd never end…"

The man who came to tune our piano was not impressed, sharing his view that it was gimmicky and not a quality piano to learn to play on. It certainly was better than cardboard.

Daddy explored The Royal Conservatory of Music to find a more qualified piano teacher for me. The conservatory was affiliated with the University of Toronto and was known for its exceptional reputation. It was where Glenn Gould, their most outstanding pupil, had studied. Daddy found Laurel Robinson. She was just like her name, melodic and pleasant, with a true passion for piano. Once a week, after school, I took the subway down to 273 Bloor Street West and climbed the steps to enter this magnificent historical building. Walking down those hallowed halls to the little room where Miss Robinson held her private classes was a sensual delight of sound. All kinds of musicians were having lessons behind the many closed doors, and strains of opera singers and pianists wafted through the air all around me, creating a warm lyrical feeling. I started to believe that perhaps I could become a pianist.

Most weeks Daddy met me outside the conservatory after my lesson. We would walk down Bloor Street together, deciding on where to have our dinner. Being alone with Daddy away from home, eating at a restaurant, was a special treat. We didn't eat anywhere fancy – usually Harvey's or Swiss Chalet – but the taste of the salty, crispy golden french fries we'd gobbled down while talking about our day was feast enough for me. Those were the days.

Chapter 25
Blossoming Sexuality

THE PEOPLE IN MY FAMILY WERE ALWAYS LEAVING. I WAS USUALLY in the house alone, only the dog accompanying me, while everyone else went out. Wendy and Daddy were now both dating, so they were out every Friday and Saturday night. There was a view of our driveway from the upstairs bathroom window. I often went up there when I heard a car pull in. I would partially open one of the slats on the white-painted shutters to watch unseen who was coming and going. I saw Daddy opening the passenger door and tucking in some young attractive woman, laughing and sharing pleasantries as they prepared for a night out. I also saw him making out in the driveway at the end of the night, pressing his body against this same woman, while they both leaned up against the car. It was gross to see my father doing this, yet I couldn't turn away. It was like watching the reality-TV show *The Bachelor*. It's embarrassing to watch the contestants make fools of themselves, yet it's also riveting, a guilty pleasure.

As cars pulled away taking Wendy or Daddy to places unknown, I felt a pang of loneliness. I was too old to need a sitter, yet still too young to have a boyfriend of my own. When I was alone with our dog Tina, the house felt hollow, silent, and empty. All the fun was happening somewhere else.

I did, however, love Martin Hambrock. Perhaps he could be my boyfriend. Martin was a good-looking twelve-year-old boy in my grade six class. He had brown eyes, brown wavy hair, and a constant tan. He was shy, polite, and seemed much more mature than the other boys. He spoke with a stutter. He lived in the valley, so we often walked home from school together.

In my diary dated March 27, 1969, I wrote:

> Martin came over after school today and gave me a present for my birthday —posters. The big one says LOVE on it. The card says, "I love you so much it hurts well actually it's more of an itch. Happy Birthday Marsha. Yours, all yours. Love and kisses (lots of them), Martin."
>
> Well, it made me sick, so I threw the card out. I dislike him now.
>
> P.S. He wouldn't leave when he was here.

April 7, 1969

Dear Diary,

I now like Martin. Not as much as I used to though. The whole school knows about the card and I don't like Martin. Martin also found out that I don't like him as much.

May 20, 1969

Dear Diary,

Yesterday was firecracker day. Martin walked me home from the park. I really like Martin again, but at times he makes me so mad.

September 1969

Dear Diary,

I wrote Martin a letter saying I didn't like him anymore and now I'm really sorry I sent it. You see, when he left to go to school in Switzerland, I wasn't here, so he went and said good-bye to Susan Stinson and he kissed her. So, I'm really jealous, that's all there is to it. I wrote him and said I knew that he liked Susan. I don't know if he really does. I wish I hadn't sent the letter. Every day I come home and check the mail to see if he has written me back yet. I like Martin a lot and I wish I hadn't sent him that stupid letter. I think I like him. When he's away I miss him, but when he's here, I don't care. I guess I take advantage of him. I wish Martin wrote me back a letter saying that he liked me and not Susan at all. I think I've lost Martin for good now. If he does write back and says he still likes me, then I'll tell him I wrote the letter to see how he would respond and that I was really jealous and didn't want to admit it, so instead I wrote that letter to see if he really liked me.

In March 1970, I wrote Martin another letter, telling him that I still did like him and that I was sorry. Martin wrote me back and sent a real nice letter. It made me so happy.

Love seems complicated.

Chapter 26
Wedding Bells

THE YEAR I TURNED FOURTEEN, ALL THREE MEMBERS OF MY FAMILY got married.

Daddy didn't venture far and married Brenda, his office secretary.

Connie, who was twenty-two, married Saul. I found out that the term *pinned* meant a promise of engagement, so they had made this promise quite a while ago.

Wendy married a solid, reliable Jewish man named Steve, who didn't resemble any of the adventurous men she had dated before. It was obvious he was crazy about her while she didn't seem as enamoured with him.

"Steve, can you drive me and Ellen to the mall?" Wendy asked regularly.

"Sure, babe, I'd be happy to go to the mall with the two of you."

"Well, can you just drop us off and pick us up in two hours?"

She went through the motions, knowing that at age nineteen, this was an acceptable one-way ticket to leave home. She'd had her fill of the many women who had passed through our home, and with another stepmother about to enter our lives, she wanted out. Even though there was a six-year age difference between Wendy and me, we were close. We shared a common taste in music. We went shopping together. I knew her friends, she knew mine, and we could talk about girl stuff. We laughed at the same things and while she did tease me as her younger sister, I knew she loved me and we were family, together forever. It was comforting to have her living at home, the one constant in the ever-changing sea of women coming and going. The idea of her leaving to get married filled me with fear and panic. Who would I talk to, go to for advice, commiserate with, about all the craziness in our home life? "Don't worry, I'll still see you all the time," Wendy assured me as the impending wedding date loomed. But she would have a husband – it wouldn't be the same.

They all married for different reasons: Connie for love, Wendy for escape, and Daddy for sex. What Brenda lacked in intelligence, she made up for in sexiness. Not much of a conversationalist, she compensated by providing more to look at. Brenda's hemlines and necklines almost seemed to meet. She had short jet-black hair that was teased in the back, with long straight bangs that moved up and down slightly when she blinked. Only a few years older than Connie, Brenda looked more like Daddy's daughter than his wife.

Connie was upset that Daddy jumped the queue and married before her because Brenda then had to be included in her wedding photographs. It was a jarring juxtaposition to see the family photos from Connie's May 1971 wedding. Daddy and Saul in their black formal tuxes and bowties flanking Catherine, the virgin bride, in her high-collared, sequined white gown, while Brenda looked like Jezebel, with her voluptuous breasts plunging out of her low V-neck flowered floor-length dress.

Brenda came with a son, Kevin, who was six years old and had what you might call an energetic personality. Today it's called ADHD. It was a package deal, so both Brenda and Kevin moved in. Kevin had been living with his grandmother in Otterville, Ontario, seeing his mom only on weekends because she thought the small-town life with his grandmother – who was home during the week – was better for him. Wendy renamed the town Hooterville, since it seemed like Brenda and Kevin were hillbillies who had come from the fictitious town in the TV show *Petticoat Junction*.

STORM ORPHAN

Brenda said her mother had fed Kevin a lot of sugar and that was why he was so hyper. Kevin had grown up with sugared cereals for breakfast, candy for snacks and pop to drink, as a well as a steady diet of cartoons on TV. Daddy said that all Kevin needed was a healthy diet, as well as some clear rules to follow. Apparently, his grandmother didn't know how to say no.

A bedroom was set up in the basement for Kevin, with red carpeting, blue and white striped wallpaper, and matching bright red and blue bedspreads on the twin beds. If the overstimulating decor didn't drive Kevin crazy, then the outdoor padlock on his bedroom door would.

Chapter 27
Punishment and Padlocks

IT WAS QUITE AN ADJUSTMENT TO HAVE BRENDA AND KEVIN MOVE in. Not only did our diets change to processed, packaged, and frozen foods, but mealtimes around the dining-room table seemed to disappear altogether.

Brenda wasn't much of a cook. If she learned culinary skills from her mother, the proof was in the pudding that Kevin was fed when he lived with his grandma.

There was nothing I could connect to with Brenda. My hopes of finding a mother figure in her were non-existent. I was embarrassed by her sexy demeanour and lack of intellect. Her thinly plucked and arched eyebrows, filled in with coloured brown pencil to create an upside- down letter U, evoked a constant look of puzzlement and questioning to her face. This made it look like she never really knew what was going on, which was fitting.

Shortly after Daddy and Brenda married, we went to temple for a Yom Kippur service. Brenda had converted to Judaism to marry Daddy, but I honestly don't know how she passed and met all the requirements. Maybe Daddy just paid Rabbi Bielfeld to put her through.

We were at temple to acknowledge Yom Kippur, the holiest day of the Jewish year, a day when you are supposed to fast and repent for your sins. After the service was over, Brenda and I went to the washroom together. When we came out, it was very busy and crowded in the main foyer and hard to find Daddy in a sea of men all wearing the same black suits. We decided to get a bird's-eye view and went up the staircase to look down from the balcony that overlooked the foyer to see if we could spot him that way. As I scanned the heads of all the dark-haired men and women, I saw Daddy's head, with his wispy black hair combed over in an attempt to cover his bald spot. It was clear from this height that his efforts at concealment were unsuccessful.

"There he is," I said to Brenda, proud that I had found him so adeptly.

I headed to go down the stairs to meet him and I heard Brenda call out, "Honey!" in a high-pitched voice.

I turned back, thinking she must be joking, but no, I could see she was seriously trying to capture my dad's attention from a hundred feet away on a balcony with a sea of over one hundred and fifty people below.

"Honey!" Brenda said, a decibel lower, and a dozen or so men looked up to the balcony as the term of endearment was clearly one many other husbands responded to.

When she yelled out the third "Honey!" accompanied by a frantic wave of her right hand, I skulked down the stairs hoping no one associated me with this ignorant woman. I was embarrassed, feeling the heat in my face rise as my shame became evident. If she had yelled out "Gilbert" to draw my father's attention, that would have been better than the generic "Honey" that seemed stupid in its syrupy sweetness.

As I met up with my father before Brenda descended the staircase, I looked at his face for telltale signs of embarrassment, but he was in conversation with another man. If he felt anything, he certainly didn't show it.

Brenda found her way to us and hung quietly at my father's side, smiling while blinking her false eyelashes at the group of people who were chatting together in a semicircle. Rabbi Bielfeld joined our group and thanked everyone for coming to the service. Just before we all dispersed, Brenda found her voice and said to the rabbi, "Would you like to come to our house for lunch today?" There was a hush among the crowd with quizzical looks exchanged. Some people just looked downcast at the floor. Now I could see the embarrassment on Daddy's face, his eyes darting from the rabbi to the group of people around him, speechless for once in his life. Rabbi Bielfeld smiled, one of those fake smiles where your eyes don't really move but your mouth overcompensates with extra effort.

"Well," said the rabbi, "I know we are all fasting today, but I'd be happy to come to lunch another day, Brenda."

Daddy must have paid him a lot for those Judaism classes – no way Brenda passed.

Kevin and I had a different relationship than Brenda and I had. For me, it was love and hate. I could see that he was a troubled kid with so much hyper energy. He was like the Road Runner in the cartoon I used to watch, zipping and spinning all over the place. I felt sorry for him, as it was clear to me that having Brenda for a mother put him at a disadvantage. He grew up seeing her only on weekends and it was evident he had missed learning about consistency, rules, and boundaries.

When Brenda married my dad, they both tried to change Kevin's diet because they thought his sugar intake was a contributing factor to his wild behaviour. Presented with a healthy breakfast to replace his Cocoa Puffs, Kevin screamed and demand his sugary dosage for his morning meal.

"I want my Cocoa Puffs!" he would yell at the top of his lungs, grabbing the spoon with his little fist, banging it on the kitchen table in defiance.

"Now, honey, we talked about this, remember? We are going to try to eat healthy now," said Brenda.

Maybe Kevin was born addicted to sugar, since Brenda was always sipping Pepsi all day long. She couldn't have been a good role model.

When Kevin's demands escalated, my father would step in, asserting the male voice, which he thought was lacking in Kevin's life.

"Stop this and eat your breakfast," Daddy ordered. "Or you will go to your room."

This method often backfired, with Kevin becoming even more adamant and belligerent. Daddy would pick him up while he yelled and screamed, his limbs frantically flipping in all directions like a fish on a hook. I watched in disgust and horror while my father took Kevin down to the basement to his psychedelic room, locking him in with a padlock on the outside of his bedroom door. He had to make a quick getaway to make it to the door because Kevin, full of adrenalin, would make a beeline to his exit before Daddy got there. The sound of Kevin banging on that door and crying to get out was painful. I could see that he needed adult authority to tame him, but this just seemed plain cruel.

Daddy sometimes asked me to babysit Kevin when they went out. Feeling I had no choice, I did so reluctantly. On one of the days Daddy and Brenda had gone out for an afternoon, I felt sorry for Kevin because they didn't seem to take him out much, and he had no friends. I decided I'd take him to the library, thinking he might enjoy the quiet peacefulness of that setting and we could borrow some books to take home. He liked me and looked up to me – his fourteen-year-old stepsister – and I thought I understood him better than his Pepsi-addicted mother and my controlling father.

I asked Kevin if he wanted to go with me and he was thrilled, jumping up and down like a jack-in-the-box at the opportunity for an adventure. I carefully explained to him about the rules: how to travel on a bus, and the expectations for quiet in a library setting. He nodded his small head up and down to demonstrate his understanding, his impish little eyes looking just like Brenda's (minus the heavy black eyeliner and false eyelashes), opened wide with anticipation and excitement.

I was pleased that I was embarking on this journey. I knew how it felt to be left out, abandoned, and un-mothered, and thought I'd save this little boy by giving him the affection and recognition he so badly needed. I also wanted to show Daddy and Brenda that the way to manage the wildness in Kevin was through love and attention, not punishment and padlocks.

We set off on our journey to the library hand in hand, making the long walk out of the valley to the bus stop. I assumed Kevin had been on a bus before, since his mom had lived at Bayview and Eglinton and used Toronto transit as her mode of transportation. The bus arrived and we chose to sit on the long bench-seats at the front. Kevin got on his knees and turned around so he could face out the wide window and watch the scenery pass by on the street. I held my head high, proud of what I'd already accomplished, thinking about the story I would tell my father later about my ability to manage what they clearly could not.

A little lost in my daydreams, I hadn't noticed that Kevin had popped off his seat and was walking down the middle of the bus. He was talking to other passengers as he made his way rolling from side to side with the movement of the bus.

I went to retrieve him and said, "Come on, Kevin, let's go sit down. It's not safe to stand while the bus is moving."

"No, I don't wanna sit down," he replied, the twinkle in his brown eyes daring me to challenge him.

I went for his hand and he slipped away like a cat on the run, emitting a deep hysterical laugh. Passengers were now watching this scene and I became self-conscious of my inability to manage the situation, my customary flush of red clearly visible in my face. I didn't want to raise my voice and turn into my father, yet I really didn't know what to do. While I was weighing my options, Kevin moved to the back of the bus and was doing something that was causing passengers to look away and some were admonishing him. I raced to the back, grabbing the long silver poles to steady myself, and saw that Kevin had his pants down. He had pulled out his little six-year-old penis and was waving it around at all the passengers, repeating, "How do you like this? How do you like this?"

"Kevin, stop that!" was all I had in my arsenal.

His giddy laugh, which accompanied his flashing, was almost as concerning as the behaviour. Not knowing what else to do, I managed to get us both off at the next stop. We turned around and walked back home. We never made it to the library.

I was shocked, full of fear, and realized I couldn't handle him on my own at all. I was no better than my dad, or Brenda for that matter. At that moment, I hated the little bugger and thought why couldn't he just behave? Couldn't he see I was being nice, trying to help him?

When we got home, I punished him by putting him in his room, padlock secured.

CHAPTER 28
Wherever You Walk

I STILL HAVE DREAMS — MORE LIKE NIGHTMARES — THAT I'M GOING to my piano lesson with Miss Robinson and I haven't practised. Daddy would remind me every day to practise, inducing guilt if I hadn't followed through with the required preparation. Playing piano never came naturally to me. If I was at a party and there was a piano, my friends would say, "Play us something, Marsh." When I refused, they would pester me, urging with even more force. The truth was that I couldn't just pick up and play any old song. I had to learn a piece note by note, using sheet music. It was work. It demanded time, discipline, and effort. However, I did feel a sense of satisfaction when I had mastered a song, learning not only the notes and pace but also the emotion behind the piece. Miss Robinson was always encouraging me to "feel the music." She would belt out the notes in her melodic voice and encourage me to do the same. "Sing the notes out loud, Marsha."

I was shy, self-conscious, and felt totally uncomfortable doing this in front of her. At home I could sing, especially when I played from the sheet music of Joni Mitchell or Carole King. But I wanted to please Miss Robinson so I made a feeble attempt.

"Good, now try it again and sing loudly with gusto."

I admired Miss Robinson's zest and earnestness, but my appreciation and appetite weren't as ravenous as hers. When I was twelve years old, she suggested that I audition for one of the student recitals she held several times a year. I reluctantly agreed. I was taking piano theory lessons once a week as well as my classes with her, and she felt I had progressed enough to perform in front of a live audience.

"You can invite your family to attend. It's a wonderful evening with a range of performances by students from several different studios," Miss Robinson rang out in her singsong voice.

The process of being able to perform at a recital involved going down to The Royal Conservatory of Music on Bloor Street to audition in front of the esteemed Dr. Ochtorlony. He was a master pianist and conductor whom Miss Robinson often quoted and talked about. It was evident that she admired Dr. O, as she called him. He had some high position at the Conservatory and was an imposing man. He was tall and thin with a wrinkly face framed by square black glasses. He was as serious as Laurel was enchanting. Miss Robinson was single and I don't know if Dr. O was married or not, but I envisioned how a romantic liaison between the two of them would be mutually beneficial. His serious demeanour lightened by Miss Robinson's joie de vivre and Miss Robinson, I thought, could use a little more gravitas. What beautiful music they could create together.

I practised my two pieces for the audition with Dr. O: *Allegretto in G* by Haydn and *Adante* by Kruger. I transcribed the audition results scribbled in Dr. Ochtorolony's illegible handwriting on the official orange report card:

> *Clear, promising playing of Allegretto- Grade B.*
> *Some confusion in the Adante-Grade A.*

I wasn't sure why I got a higher grade in the *Adante* because I had made some errors, but Miss Robinson assured me that grades were not lower due to mistakes. I must have done a good job on the interpretation. She decided I should choose the *Allegretto* for the recital, since I was obviously more confident playing that and I eagerly agreed.

I was no longer going downtown for my lessons with Miss Robinson because she had moved to North Toronto, purchasing a home that was very close to where we lived. She rented studio space from a very old woman who reminded me of a character in an English fairy tale. She was a teeny-tiny woman who lived in a teeny-tiny house. This ancient woman would shuffle her way to the front door to let you in to wait in the small hallway for your lesson. She had such a severe hunchback that she couldn't look up to meet your eyes when she talked to you. There really wasn't any chance of conversation anyway, since she was very hard of hearing. She had a special device on the receiver of her telephone to help her hear the calls. If I used her phone to ask Daddy to come and pick me up after class, it would screech at a high pitch, almost causing a hearing impairment for the user. I don't know how Miss Robinson found this woman, but it was clear she was providing company, music, and joy to someone who had literally a very small world.

My entire family attended the evening student concert held at the recital hall at The Royal Conservatory of Music: Daddy, Brenda, Wendy, Steve, Connie, Saul, even Lynn, who was our housekeeper at the time.

There was a clearly stated rule that all friends and family members were to remain for the entire concert, since it would be rude to leave and not hear each performer's piece. It was a lengthy program, with forty different students playing a range of songs, culminating in the senior students playing the most challenging pieces by Rachmaninoff and Beethoven at the end of the recital. My personal audience of seven took up most of the middle row. I was grateful to have my anxiety relieved by playing my *Allegretto in G major* near the beginning of the program so I could then enjoy the rest of the evening.

About halfway through the concert, a woman in her twenties with very pale white skin and long curly black hair stepped up on stage and clasped her hands in front of her chest in preparation to sing. The pianist accompanying her played a few chords of introduction and then the soprano began singing Handel's "Where'er you walk." I could hear my father making an odd coughing noise. I looked down our row past the others to view Daddy, who was at the end. I could see his telltale shoulders bobbing up and down. He was laughing and trying to cover up the noise he was making by coughing. I tried to send a scowl down his way, but his head was down, eyes to the floor. No sooner had I turned away when I felt movement in our row. Daddy was now standing up and leaving the room in the middle of this woman's performance! As he pushed the doors open to exit, each member of my family stood up and followed him like a set of dominoes moving in succession. Ashamed, not knowing what to do, I followed.

We all caught up to Daddy, who was around the corner from the recital hall out of earshot, laughing uncontrollably. He looked up, surprised to see all of us.

"What are you all doing?" he said between bouts of laughter.

"What happened to you?" I asked.

"I'm sorry, honey, but as soon I saw that woman clasp her hands and then that opera stuff came out, I couldn't help it. It gets me every time. I just find it so comical. I didn't mean for you all to follow me, I just had to get out. Why did you all leave?"

Brenda was the first to respond. "I heard you coughing, and just wondered if you were all right."

"I don't know, I saw you both leave, so I thought I'd better follow too," said Lynn.

And so it went. I worried about what I was going to tell Miss Robinson at my next piano class. I was so humiliated. Thankfully she never brought it up, nor did I.

Eventually, it came to be a family story, one of those memories we shared over meals at the dining-room table. Someone, usually Wendy, would bring it up. "Remember that time we all followed Daddy out of Marsha's piano recital during that opera song, 'Where'er you walk?'" she'd ask, laughing at the irony of it all. It was a comfort to know that, however wacky my family was, we were all in it together.

Chapter 29
New Horizons

JUNIOR HIGH WAS WHERE I FORMED MY NEW FAMILY. MY SOCIAL world widened and I met a new group of friends who were more diverse than the public-school kids I had grown up with. I escaped my lonely, crazy household and hung out at my friends' houses during my free time.

Kathy Sniderman, Carla Schneider, and Renee Seligman were all Jewish like me. They lived above the valley in a newer subdivision, in a neighbourhood we called Fairmeadow, which was the name of the feeder public school for our junior high, St. Andrew's.

I had the most in common with Kathy Sniderman, who had two older sisters the same age as Connie and Wendy. She had no father. He died when she was young. Kathy also had a stepparent, an older interesting man named Sydney who looked like an artist with his long white hair and thick black round-rimmed glasses. It turned out he *was* an artist. There were large modern paintings hanging on the wall at Kathy's house and they were all done by Sydney.

Now there were boys in my life as well. Stirrings emerged in my body and brain that I had never felt before. While I had felt something for Martin Hambrock, I was pretending, or trying on love. These boys were the real deal. A look or a comment from Dave Ellins, Kip McCaskill, or Cobby Gareau sent my heart pounding. I didn't really know that much about sex, other than observing the antics that went on in my house, which kind of repulsed me.

No one ever told me anything about sex, my body, how you got pregnant or, for that matter, avoided pregnancy. Connie had left a folder on the desk in my bedroom with a booklet inside that had the heading *All about Menstruation*. I didn't even know what that word meant. I looked through the booklet and wondered when this strange thing was going to happen to me. When I did get my first period, the day after my fourteenth birthday, Wendy joked about it and said, "You are a woman now, Marcia," a nickname she had given me based on the commercial jingle for Lancia spaghetti. She would replace the brand name Lancia with Marcia and sing, "Marcia, Marcia, in the blue and white package, Marcia, Marcia, mmmm tastes good."

"Don't call me that," I pleaded unsuccessfully. I sang back "Wencia, Wencia," but it never had the same effect on her.

Connie, who was clearly playing the motherly role, gave me advice when I wanted to transition from the boat-like sanitary pads to the tampons she'd left on my desk. I called her on the phone. "How do I insert a tampon? I've read the instructions in the box, but it keeps coming out."

"Get the radio and put it into the bathroom, so you can relax, then find the middle hole and insert."

I hung up the phone, even more confused. How many holes did I have?

There was no one I could really talk to about this. I persisted and after going through a frustrating experience using half a box of Tampax, I eventually found the right hole. Then there was the issue of buying the tampons. I didn't do the shopping – Daddy did – nor did I have any money. What to do? We always had a running shopping list in the kitchen that sat on the arborite counter beside the telephone. I decided to add tampons to the list. Magically, a blue box of Tampax appeared in my upstairs bathroom every month.

STORM ORPHAN

The boys who were my age had an energetic, carefree attitude that was magnetic and appealing. My group of friends hung out in in the local park just across from St. Andrew's.

Rye and ginger ale was my choice of beverage. It was easy for me to access because I could siphon off small amounts from the magnums of Canadian Club that were in our basement, the ones my dad received as Christmas gifts from business associates. When they became low or empty, I just filled them with water. Our housecleaner, Henry, had taught me this trick.

Getting drunk was liberating. I lost my inhibitions, my shyness, and felt comfortable with everyone, even the boys. We told stories, laughed together, and in those moments we were one. Being drunk was the great equalizer. Who your family was didn't matter. Nobody knew much about each other's family. It wasn't important. We all thought our parents were clueless, just roommates we had to endure living with until we could be independent and free.

Linda Feingold was another Jewish friend who had recently moved into the valley. She lived just up the hill from the judge who had driven Leigh, Tori, and me to school a few times. Her family seemed wackier than mine. Well, really it was her mom, Abby, who seemed crazy. She had two moods: syrupy sweet or scary angry. Our families went to the same temple. Mrs. Feingold seemed to like me, and when I was at their house, she often asked about my dad and how he was. I had seen Linda's mom angry when Linda and I were caught shoplifting at Fairview Mall on Yom Kippur. We had lied and told our parents we were going to Temple together and instead we went to the mall and stole a whole bunch of things, including lip gloss, earrings, record albums, and candy. The mall security guard caught us, took us into a room, and made us call our parents to come pick us up. Since it was the middle of the day, Daddy was at work and couldn't leave – no more Yom Kippur services for him. Linda's mom came and she yelled at us in the car all the way home.

"Marsha Barrett, how could *you* do this? Wait until I tell your father and on Yom Kippur of all things. You two girls will be punished for this. Linda, you just wait until we get home."

I was more scared of Mrs. Feingold than of what my father would do because I'd heard him say, "That Abby Feingold is a crazy bitch." I knew I could work this into my defending argument with him somehow.

Linda had a younger brother who seemed a little like Kevin. He was also punished by being put into his room (minus the padlock). Linda's parents were divorced. I had never met anyone whose parents were divorced. Linda's stepdad, Larry, was a boring, slightly overweight guy, with thick-rimmed glasses; a doctor, who looked much older than Abby. Jeff, Linda's biological dad, was young, good-looking, and the antithesis of Larry. He drove a flashy red sports car. Not so dependable, though. Mrs. Feingold was often visibly angry at him and yelled about all the things he didn't do. "He never shows up on time, if he shows up at all. Your dad never pays child support."

I felt sorry for Linda, as this was her dad after all, and I could tell she loved him.

Linda's grandmother lived with them and this also seemed unusual to me. She said her grandmother was Ojibway, which made Linda part "Indian." That was the term we used then.

Linda's striking looks reflected her colourful family. With her long, thick auburn hair, parted down the middle, her olive skin, and a smattering of freckles, she was an exotic blend of both Jewish and Indigenous heritage. Linda and I engaged in risky adventures, the shoplifting being just one of many. Ultimately, we had to go back to each store we had stolen from, apologize, and return every single item. It was extremely embarrassing and repetitive. Having to go back to each shopkeeper, tell our story in front of Mrs. Feingold, and be admonished multiple times was humiliating. I don't know why we stole that stuff. At the time, it was thrilling and we were gratified that we could get away with it. Most of the things we stole were gifts we were going to give to our friends.

In hindsight, I can see that it was a desperate cry for attention. Linda and I were both adrift in our sea of dysfunctional family dynamics.

Chapter 30
A Kindred Spirit

TORI SAID SHE PICKED ME OUT TO BE HER FRIEND IN OUR GRADE eight English class with Mr. Butters. She had moved around a lot, living in Sarnia and Edmonton, and could tell which of the kids she wanted to hang out with. I looked "cool," she said. I was thrilled at receiving this compliment. It was the image I was trying to project.

In junior high, I traded in my Julie Andrews straight hair cut for an afro-type perm. No more goody two shoes for me. Mary Poppins never did show up, and speaking out seemed like the way to get what you wanted. I was feeling bold and brave. I saw images of Angela Davis with her large puffball of an afro. Her outspoken fight for justice for blacks was inspiring. While I was a privileged white teenager living in suburbia, I was tapping into a newfound anger and saw how valuable this could be. It felt good not to care so much anymore about what people thought. I had been a good quiet girl, behaved nicely, and where had it gotten me? Adults in my family had come and gone like a revolving door, always letting me down. I wanted my look on the outside to match how I felt on the inside.

Daddy initially said I could get a perm, but after talking to a few mothers in the valley who said it was expensive and unnecessary for a girl who was only fourteen, he reneged on his promise. One night after I'd gone to bed, he left me a note on the kitchen table to inform me there would be no money for my perm. How feeble, I thought, that he couldn't tell me to my face. I was gaining a newfound power in our relationship too because I saw through his sham of a marriage and often called him and Brenda out on some of the ways they were mistreating Kevin. I realized I could speak my mind and Daddy, just as he wasn't sure what to do with Kevin, wasn't sure what to do with me. I left my own note in return on the kitchen table – a full page and a half – outlining how it was important to keep promises made, highlighting some of his own personal expenses that were extravagant: cigars from Havana, suits that were tailor-made. The next morning, I woke up and my note was gone, replaced with several crisp twenty-dollar bills.

Tori said she was drawn to my afro perm and gold wire-rimmed John Lennon glasses. I didn't think it was cool at all to have to wear glasses. I had discovered in grade four why I always had to sit at the front of the class to see the chalkboard. I was near-sighted. Getting glasses changed everything and I was shocked when I put my first pair on, discovering that this was how everyone saw things all the time. It was like I had been seeing the world through a haze of fog and suddenly the mist lifted and I could see clear, sharp details. I could also move to the back of the class.

When we were assigned to complete a partnered project in Mr. Butters's class to analyze the lyrics of a song, Tori came up to me and asked, "Do you want to be partners?"

I only knew her as the new kid in class, who lived in the valley down the street from us, on Green Valley Road. Tori looked different, like she came from somewhere else, since she didn't seem to care about the style all the girls were wearing: bell bottoms or extra-wide elephant pants with textured tight bubble tops, which really did look like the bubble wrap used to package fragile objects in boxes. She wore loose plaid tops tucked into straight-leg, button-fly Levi's jeans.

She looked stylish in her own way, with her blond pageboy cut, but more than that she looked comfortable in her clothes and in her skin.

"Sure, I'll be your partner," I said somewhat shyly because this was a new experience for me, to meet someone who had moved from somewhere else.

"What song do you think we should pick?" Tori asked as we fell into step walking home together after school one day.

Trying to act clever, I thought I'd throw out a song by a fringe artist who wasn't on the pop charts, someone who Tori wouldn't know. Wendy had exposed me to a wide range of music and I had grown to love Laura Nyro, a songwriter not widely known but who had made hits for other artists such as The 5th Dimension and David Clayton Thomas.

"How about a Laura Nyro song?" I tossed out nonchalantly, not making eye contact but checking Tori's reaction with a sidelong glance.

"What?" She stopped in her tracks and turned to look me in the eye. With her own blue eyes ablaze, she said, "You know Laura Nyro? I love her music! Oh my gosh, I can't believe you know Laura Nyro."

I was impressed that Tori knew her too but didn't want to show it and give away my excitement as easily as she had. I wanted to hold my cards a little closer to my non-existent chest so, containing my own surprise, I said, "Yup, I really like her music."

My heart beat a little faster as we continued the long walk home to the valley, excited to get to know this new girl. I had lost my bosom buddy Susan Stinson to private school, and while I had quite a few friends, none of them listened to Laura Nyro.

Tori could be the kindred spirit I so needed and craved. When she asked if I wanted to come over to her house on Green Valley Road and start working on the project, I immediately said yes.

This might be the green valley that would lead me into greener pastures.

Chapter 31
Hash Hijinks

Tori, Linda, and I had decided that we wanted to branch out beyond rye & ginger. My stockpile was also becoming depleted. I knew Wendy smoked pot and I thought she would be a safe person to ask about how to purchase or maybe even supply it. So after school one day, the three of us made a phone call to my sister from Linda's house. I knew Wendy was at home preparing dinner for Steve and no one else was at home at Linda's, so the timing was good. At Linda's house, each of us could be on a different phone at the same time. Tori and I chose two phones in different rooms in the basement while Linda was on the phone upstairs in her parents' bedroom.

"Okay, pick up," I yelled, so Tori and Linda knew when I had finished dialling Wendy's number on the rotary phone. With the sound of the phone ringing over our respective receivers, the three of us said "Hi" to one another.

We heard Wendy pick up. "Hello?" I had planned with Wendy ahead of time to make this call, so we could get right to the business of discussing a pot purchase.

"Hi. Wendy. Tori and Linda are also on the line."

"Hi, gals," said Wendy nonchalantly, as if selling pot was no big deal to her. My heart was pounding so loudly, I thought everyone could hear it through the receiver, since what we were about to do was illegal and we were talking about it in Linda's house. What if, God forbid, her mother found out?

"So how much does it cost to buy a dime of hash?" I asked Wendy. I knew enough about the terms of weight used (nickel, dime, and quarter-pound) to sound knowledgeable.

"Well, a dime of hash would be about…is it hash or marijuana you want?"

"I think we want hash, right, girls?" I heard Linda and Tori reply "Yes" in unison, but I also heard a click on the line, like someone else had picked up the phone. Tori heard it too because she immediately said, "What was that?"

Tori was more scared than any of us, since her dad was pretty strict and Linda's mom terrified her. Before we could respond, I heard Linda's mom yelling. She was upstairs in the kitchen, the same floor as Linda.

"What the hell is going on here? You're making a drug deal?" Mrs. Feingold's voice reverberated throughout the entire house. I quickly hung up on Wendy and raced upstairs. Tori was right behind me. Mrs. Feingold was in a blind rage in the kitchen, her normally wide, smooth ageless face all contorted with furrows and wrinkles. I tried to make out what she was saying, while the blood from my heart pounded in my ears. The hallway and access to the front door to escape was behind her.

"You again, Marsha, involved in illegal activity! You little bitches wait right here while I call the police. Don't move."

I looked behind me at Tori, her face frozen in fear, our worst nightmare come true. Linda didn't look worried, since this nightmare was her daily reality. We waited in the kitchen while Mrs. Feingold picked up the phone and began to dial. She glared at us, slammed down the receiver, and yelled at Tori and me.

"You girls, get out of my house right now! What are you still doing here?"

Tori and I looked at each other in panic. We had two conflicting instructions: do we stay or do we go? Adrenalin flowing and all signs pointing to flight, I raced out of the kitchen and down the hallway to the front door. Tori followed right behind me. Behind her was Mrs. Feingold, beating Tori on her back, her legs, or whatever part of her body she could reach, as she ran to keep up. I got out quickly and turned around to see Tori fumbling with the screen door handle. She kept pushing the little silver knob to release the door, but it seemed to be stuck. It was like one of those dramatic movie scenes, when there are seconds left before the ticking time bomb is about to explode. Finally, the door released. Not stopping to look behind us, we ran at full speed down the driveway, all the way down the large hill that Linda's house was perched on, until we reached a street where we were out of sight, both of us panting, out of breath, and crying with fear as well as relief that we had escaped.

Tori couldn't stop crying and trembling from fear but also shame. Her straight-legged, Levi's button-up jeans were soaked in pee.

I decided to take on the purchasing of hash as a solo job.

Chapter 32
Fault Line

THE HONEYMOON PERIOD — IF THERE EVER WAS ONE — APPEARED to be over with Daddy and Brenda. They were either screaming and yelling at each other or giving each other the silent treatment and not talking at all. Kevin's behaviour wasn't really improving. Daddy and Brenda took him to meet with a psychologist, a friend of Wendy and Steve's, named Vern. Vern said that Kevin was mentally ill, that he lived in a fantasy world. "If he doesn't have psychiatric treatment by the time he's ten years old, he could become very violent," warned Vern. He recommended that he go to a special school. I felt badly for Kevin, but he also irritated me. I was tired of having to take on the responsibility of looking after him.

Once when Kevin went skating with his class on a school trip, he fell, requiring a visit to the hospital to get stitches. Since Daddy and Brenda weren't around, his school contacted me to come and pick him up. Mr. Meek, my grade eight history teacher, drove me and Kevin to the hospital. *How embarrassing*, I wrote in my diary. When Kevin was sick, sometimes I stayed home to watch him. I didn't mind missing school and getting to watch TV all day, but when Brenda and Daddy went out at night and I had to babysit that really bothered me because that was when all my friends were doing something fun that I had to miss.

I was in the kitchen when I found out Brenda was gone.

"Where's Brenda?" I asked Daddy one Sunday morning – or I guess it was afternoon by the time I rolled out of bed late after a Saturday night of partying with my friends.

"She left," said Daddy, looking up briefly from the *Toronto Telegram* newspaper he was reading while seated at the kitchen table drinking his Ovaltine. The aroma of malt and chocolate filled the kitchen with a soothing sense of comfort. "A lot better than coffee," Daddy always said. He prided himself on a healthy diet of lean meat, greens, and an evening ritual of Metamucil to keep his bowels regular.

"Gone where? Shopping?"

"No, gone for good," Daddy said with little or no emotion, barely even making eye contact with me, his attention focused on the newspaper.

"What do you mean?" I stammered. "She's not coming back?"

It was clear that life with Kevin was challenging, and while I didn't think much of Brenda, this was so sudden, so final, a huge blow like another death had happened. "What about all Brenda's stuff, her clothes? And Kevin, he's gone too?"

"Brenda packed up all her clothes and yes, of course she took Kevin with her. They are both gone and they aren't coming back."

Why did she leave? Will I see her again? I had a million questions, but it was clear from Daddy's expressionless face and minimal communication that no more details were forthcoming. Like the pictures of Mommy removed from the walls after her death, the silence and shame that lingered in our home after Carol died, now this third marriage too was over. While it had ended differently, the outcome was the same. I was left to move on with many unanswered questions.

I sat down at the kitchen table, silently trying to absorb this new loss, and was filled with a grief I couldn't quite name. It wasn't like I loved Brenda and she hadn't died, but another pivotal person, a third "mother" in my life who I never got a chance to say goodbye to, was gone.

Daddy and Brenda had been married only two years, and while I admit that having Kevin leave was somewhat of a relief, the sudden loss of whatever semblance of a family we'd had together made me feel like I was living on a fault line and the Earth's tectonic plates had shifted once again.

Chapter 33
Déjà Vu

I DIDN'T KNOW THAT BRENDA HAD TRIED TO KILL HERSELF. LIKE Carol, she had attempted to take sleeping pills in the middle of the night so she didn't have to wake up to her miserable life ever again. Wendy told me this much later, when I was an adult. At the time of Brenda's suicide attempt, I was asleep upstairs in my bedroom, oblivious to the chaos that was going on one floor below.

My sister said it was like watching a scene unfold from a movie she had watched before but with a different leading lady. Wendy happened to be sleeping over – Steve was away – and she was in the den late at night with her best friend Arlene, watching television with the door closed, when she heard some noise and commotion coming from Daddy and Brenda's downstairs bathroom. She heard Daddy shout, "What the hell are you doing?" Since they often fought, yelling wasn't that unusual, but it was 3:00 in the morning. There was something in Daddy's tone that caused Wendy to open the den door, go down the hallway, and have a look.

There they both were in the bathroom, an opened bottle of pills spread on the counter and floor. It appeared Brenda had already taken some. Daddy was in a panic and it scared Wendy to see our father out of control like that. Not knowing what to do, Wendy called Connie, who could always be counted on to deal with a family crisis. She had, after all, dealt with this situation before.

Connie called Rabbi Bielfeld to come over in the middle of the night to help guide them. He, too, had been through this and counselled Daddy after Carol killed herself. There was then a trip to the hospital to have Brenda's stomach pumped, she survived, and a vow of silence was taken by all, making sure that this also went into the family vault of secrets.

I was shocked when I found out in my twenties about Brenda's suicide attempt. It made me question many things. How could it be that Daddy had two wives, Carol *and* Brenda, who both wanted to end their lives? What had happened to these young women – they were both only in their thirties – to cause them to make such a choice? Was there some unconscious pattern in my father's family history that he was replicating?

In later years as an adult, when I read, reflected, and eventually sought out the support of a therapist to examine the impact of death and loss in my life, something she said about suicide resonated with me.

"No one person is to blame for suicide. People kill themselves because they want to stop the pain. They often see no way out of their agony and have no hope for the future."

As a child, I wasn't told the truth about how Carol died, or Brenda's attempt, so I never blamed myself or my father, but this explanation helped me make sense of something that had previously been beyond my comprehension. How could life be so bad that someone would choose to kill themselves? Now an adult, I see that hope – for oneself, for change, for a future – is the fuel that propels us all forward. No matter how lonely and sad my days were, I always had hope that things would get better.

I never allowed myself to feel pain from the losses I experienced in my family. I didn't cry, show grief, or mourn, but moved forward and carried on. These were the lessons I learned in my family, the world I lived in, and I was proud of my toughness and resiliency. If someone asked about my family, I would list the deaths and losses as if they were items on a shopping list.

During my first visit with a therapist, after I had become a mother myself, she asked me about my own mother. I recited my history to her.

"How sad," she said.

I sobbed with wild, reckless abandon. I was a tsunami erupting on the shoreline. No one had ever responded to me with such simple empathy. I was thirty years old.

I now feel compassion for my father, since he had so many challenges, when all he really was looking for was a partner, a wife he could love. Like most teenagers, I never considered my father's feelings. I didn't really think he had feelings at all, certainly none as important as mine.

In hindsight, I do regret that I, too, caused him so much pain.

Chapter 34
To Ski or Not to Ski

WHILE INITIALLY TERRIFYING, I AM GRATEFUL THAT DADDY taught me how to ski. Similar to his swimming lessons, he ascribed to the philosophy that rather than take time for a gradual entry into the sport, it was best to snowplow right in. I was five or six years old when he decided I was ready to learn. Connie and Wendy had been skiing for several years under his tutelage and enjoyed the regular weekend visits to Blue Mountain in Collingwood. I was eager to be included in these father-daughter outings. My mother could ski, but didn't enjoy it, so she was likely glad to get some time to herself.

At the top of the mountain, with my little wooden skis strapped on, Daddy put me between his legs, bent over, wrapped his arms around my waist (no poles required), and said "Okay, boobie, let's go."

I looked down from what seemed like Mount Everest, at the tiny stick-like figures of people below, and became rigid with fear. "I don't want to go down. It's too high."

"I have you. I won't let you go. We're going to go slowly down this hill together. Just keep the tips of your skis touching, so they look like a piece of pizza."

I started crying. "No, I don't want to! I'm scared."

Daddy, ignoring my tears and panic, moved us forward and began to traverse the hill in a snowplow, with his long skis spread perfectly apart, while mine slid all over the bumpy granular snow. Once set in motion, there was no turning back.

"Bend your knees, keep your skis on the ground against mine."

I followed his instructions as if my very survival depended on it. Halfway down the hill, my dread subsiding, Daddy said, "You're skiing! Look up, look away from your skis. Do you see the view?"

Out beyond the skiers at the base of the mountain was a huge expanse of blue water that went on as far as my eye could see. Daddy said it was Georgian Bay. In that moment I forgot about my skis, my wobbly knees, my tense body, and felt myself swept away in a fluid motion down the hill, as if the vista itself was pulling us in closer to have a look. We were almost airborne. A blanket of quiet surrounded us, punctuated only by the swishing sound of the skis on the snow. It was both peaceful and exhilarating. Unlike swimming, this was a sport I took to right away.

After Brenda moved out, we went on a family ski holiday to Mount Tremblant. Connie and Saul, Wendy and Steve, and Daddy and I all piled into our station wagon to make the long drive to Quebec. We stayed at the Cuttle's Tremblant Club. Originally a log family home, Jim and Betty Cuttle transformed it into an inn with thirty rooms. The rustic bedrooms with fireplaces were a treat to stay in. As was Daddy's way, we skied from the time the lifts opened in the morning until they closed.

There was a lot of snow and it was often bitterly cold in Quebec in December. One day it was -20 degrees Fahrenheit (we didn't use metric then). It was so cold that the ski-lift operators were distributing heavy full-length vests to wear over your ski suit when you went up the chairlift and to deposit in a bin when you got off. I wanted to go inside, my face numb with cold, the scarf I had wrapped around me for warmth frozen stiff from my breath, and the snot running from my nose, but Daddy had a quota of runs we had to do in the morning before going in for lunch. The rest of the family was already inside the chalet enjoying hot chocolate by the fire; they were adults and could make their own decisions, but Daddy still had me under his control.

"One more run, then we'll go in," he said.

We went to get on the chairlift and the operator said to Daddy, "Better get her inside, looks like her chin is getting frostbite." I was glad to have this second opinion.

When we got into the toasty warm lodge that smelled of burning wood, I took off all the layers of my winter gear and felt a tingling sensation in my chin. Big red blotches of red skin slowly started to turn white as my face warmed up. The tingling turned to a burning. I definitely had frostbite. I had the privilege that day of staying in the lodge longer than the one-hour lunch Daddy usually allowed.

Trips to the Cuttle's Tremblant Club became an annual family holiday for several years. When I was fifteen, Daddy took me and Wendy on a special ski trip to Austria. Wendy was travelling in Europe at the time and met us in the picturesque town of Sölden. A charming little village set at the base of a snow-capped mountain, it looked like something out of a fairy tale. Since Wendy and I got to share a room, we managed one day of freedom from skiing, telling Daddy we were going to sleep in and would meet him on the hill later in the day. We spent the day smoking potent black hash Wendy had purchased during her European travels and eating delicious Austrian chocolate balls.

While we all groaned about Daddy's ski rules and regimen, and it sometimes seemed harsh, he was playful and fun to ski with. The sport brought us together as a family and I treasured that time. We all would tease him about his maxims: "Be the first one on the slopes in the morning. Ski until the lifts close. Look out, not down at your skis. Sing when you ski, so your body relaxes." These turned out to be metaphors that translated into important life lessons for me. Make the most of each day, don't waste precious time, look at the larger view, relax and try not to get caught up in unnecessary details.

When I was older and went off to ski with my sisters or a friend on my own and would then meet up with Daddy at the end of the day, he would always ask me, "Did you fall?"

"No, I skied perfectly, no falls."

"Well, that's not a perfect day then. Falling is good. It's a sign that you tried something new and that's how you learn."

I was headed into terrain that would result in quite a bit of tumbling.

Chapter 35
Love and Rage

WHEN DADDY WAS HOME, THEN HOME BECAME A PLACE WHERE I merely changed my clothes and slept. I spent all my waking hours, which usually included the wee small hours of the morning, out with my girlfriends, a wide circle of people, but mostly Tori, Linda, and Julie. Daddy often travelled to far-away places for business, leaving me alone from the time I was fourteen, making 77 Plymbridge party central. After Brenda moved out, Daddy had contractors come and install a small in-ground kidney-shaped pool in our backyard, which was a perfect backdrop for my summer barbecues and parties.

Perhaps Daddy invested in a pool so he could perfect his tan because he sunbathed by the pool stark naked. He lay on a lounger while holding a piece of cardboard wrapped in tinfoil up to his face to reflect the sun. In the 1970s, the goal was for white-skinned people to get as brown as they possibly could, both men and women. I remember Connie and Wendy using these same homemade sun reflectors, spreading baby oil onto their skin to roast under the sun's ultraviolet rays. Nobody knew back then that overexposure to the sun caused skin cancer. Sunblock or sunscreen was basically nonexistent. I guess that deep-baked look was in style. Knowing that my dad was laying out in our backyard exposed was gross. The first time I came outside and found Daddy naked, he quickly covered up with a towel.

Whenever Daddy said he was going to lie by the pool, I knew it wasn't safe to venture outdoors.

While Daddy's romantic life took a breather, mine blossomed. I had moved beyond the likes of Martin Hambrock, wavering between loving David Ellins and Lawrence Connolly. My diary from when I was fourteen indicates my uncertainty:

> I am beginning to think I like David better than Lawrence. I think I do. He's so nice and also I know he likes me (which helps).

My diary entry three days later:

> Dear Diary –BOY DO I LIKE DAVID !!!!! I never think about Lawrence now. It's great. David is sooo nice!! Ah, Love is grand."

Clearly, I was conflicted.

David and Lawrence both had sisters, but that was where their commonality ended.

David, who had straight light brown hair, was a sociable, talkative guy who was popular with all the girls. Lawrence had shoulder-length wavy hair and was quiet, more of a loner. People nicknamed him "the cat" as he came and went as he pleased. His mystery was alluring to me. It was convenient that Lawrence was Julie's twin brother because when I visited Julie, I could often catch Lawrence there too. We also shared the stigma of having lost a parent, although my tally was now up to three. I never felt judged or less than when I was at Julie and Lawrence's house, since their home life wasn't perfect either and there was no need to pretend about my family.

When a group of us were out at night, I would often hear another kid share her curfew time, saying, "I have to be home at midnight" and I'd feel like a neglected child. I would make up a time I had to be home to avoid my shame and feel somehow like I fit in. Daddy didn't have clear boundaries about when to be home, and usually he was out of town anyway.

I regularly skipped school and hung out in the local park, smoking cigarettes with whoever else had decided to skip either a period or a full day. Linda or Julie and I went to Fairview Mall, planned for parties we were going to have on the weekend, or just met together at our houses and listened to records. Tori couldn't skip school so easily. Her parents were more on top of things.

Sometimes I visited Wendy at the duplex she and Steve had purchased, and while Steve was at work, we went shopping together. We also worked on her house, painting the walls wild colours of purple, green, and pink. No boring white walls for her.

I asked Daddy to write me a note for a time when I had legitimately been absent from school. When my homeroom teacher, Mr. Speers, didn't ask me to submit the note, I saved it, learning to copy and perfect Daddy's quite complicated signature. This provided true freedom. I must have honed this skill pretty well because I never got caught. Daddy did ask about all my absences when he saw my report card, but I was also quite talented at coming up with bullshit stories or simply dismissing him.

I had lost all respect for my Dad at this point, and could barely stand to be around him. Some of this was likely typical teenage rebellion, but in hindsight, I think the loneliness and lack of parental boundaries translated into a feeling of abandonment. I really did want him to say no to me, to set limits and be at home more, so I upped the ante on my attitude, to see how far I could go. I wanted to be noticed. It seemed like he cared more about sex and the women he dated than he did about me. There is evidence of my growing alienation in my diary dated June 6, 1971:

Dear Diary

Was very upset tonight about this house. I hate it and can't stand living in it. I was crying and oh God, I get so depressed. Anyhow, HE came upstairs and we talked. I told him everything. I told him I don't love him and that he was a lousy father. He said I should try and get along with him. Long talk which simmered down to:

> 1. *It is impossible to live with him*
> 2. *I don't love him*
> 3. *He doesn't care*

Oh gosh, I hate this house It's sickening. I wish Wendy or Connie still lived here. It is hell living here alone. But I must try and cheer up.

My attraction to David Ellins ended in September when I found out he had fooled around with another girl during the summer. I didn't mince words when I told him, "You're nice, you're really nice. You are a low-down bastard. You make me sick. You can fuck off with that girl Mary or Belinda, or whatever the hell her name is." Perhaps I had tapped into a rage that was really targeted at my father.

My diary went on.

Everyone heard me yell at David and congratulated me for telling him off.

The encouragement emboldened me, which is not what I think I really needed at the time.

Chapter 36
Summer Sanctuaries

I WAS STILL YOUNG ENOUGH AT AGE FIFTEEN TO BE SHIPPED OFF TO summer camp. I was glad to get away from home since most of my friends weren't around in the summer: Julie went to horse camp, Tori to her island cottage on Georgian Bay, and Linda to stay at her dad's place in California. It was boring being on my own.

I had now graduated from Camp Oconto, the girls' camp where everyone was Christian, to B'nai B'rith, where everyone was Jewish. B'nai B'rith was paired with Northland, a camp for boys, so there were co-ed activities.

I didn't feel Jewish like the other kids. All the girls talked about their lavish bat mitzvahs and I barely even knew what that was. I had gone to the obligatory Sunday School at Temple Emanuel to learn about Judaism and was on the path to be confirmed, but I really didn't like it.

"I don't want to go to Sunday School anymore," I announced to Daddy after another mind-numbing morning of reading the Torah, learning about the trials and tribulations of the Jews. It didn't interest me and getting up early on Sunday morning was cutting into my slumber after a late night of partying.

"But you need to finish, Marsha, and be confirmed, like your sisters," said Daddy.

"Why? I don't believe in God or religion at all. It seems hypocritical to be confirmed when you're not a believer." I don't know if Daddy was just tired of arguing with me and it was easier to give in, or if he could see my logic. Maybe he just didn't want to have to drive me anymore, but whatever the case, I quit Sunday School. It was kind of ironic that I was even going to a Jewish camp.

B'nai B'rith wasn't a rustic wilderness camp like Oconto but was much more civilized. There was electricity in the cabins and all the girls plugged in their hair-blowers and curling irons to gussy up for the weekly Saturday-night "social" with the boys. They put on makeup and wore fancy clothes that they had packed just for these dances with the campers from Northland. I had short hair that was now straight – the perm couldn't last forever – and wasn't into makeup. I preferred the comfort and ease of being in an all-girls camp, without having to worry about boys. We could be free. We could have skinny dips.

B'nai B'rith seemed to be centred around boys. When we weren't talking about boys, then we were sneaking into their adjacent camp to spy on them. I did take a liking to one of them, Howard Chisvin, and was especially pleased when he asked me to "go around" with him. I think what I liked more than Howard himself was wearing his thick silver identity bracelet on my wrist, with the letters H O W A R D engraved on the brushed-silver nameplate. Since we were going around, he got to walk me "home" to our cabin after Saturday-night socials. This helped me to feel like I fit in, since *all* the girls in my cabin had a boyfriend.

I took part in the many activities that camp had to offer: tennis, sailing – yes, even swimming – and learned how to waterski, which was thrilling in both a good and bad way. I had to take off my glasses to waterski and I couldn't see a bloody thing. The spotter in the back of the boat would point out dangers – rocks or a nearby shoreline – and all I could make out was an arm waving around, so I waved back, thinking I was reciprocating some kind of friendliness. I did have a few close calls.

After two weeks, I came home and it was dreary. None of my friends were around and I was hanging out at Fairview and Yorkdale Malls by myself.

When Tori invited me to come to her island cottage, I was as thrilled as my dad was relieved. The white cottage surrounded by windswept pines looked like something out of a Group of Seven painting. It was located far from the mainland, in an area called Sans Souci and it truly was "without worry." Tori, along with her parents, Roy and Doris Grant, taught me a lot about life on "the bay," as they called it. While our family did have a thirty-two-foot cabin cruiser, I was young when we owned the boat and was mostly a passenger onboard. I didn't do more than help to tie up the boat, use a boat hook to fend off the cement walls in the locks we travelled through, or throw out the anchor when we stopped for a picnic somewhere on Lake Simcoe.

On Georgian Bay I learned how to drive and dock boats, as well as how to look after them. I came to understand charts and how to navigate channels to avoid rocks that were hidden just below the surface that could destroy the propeller. I drove the Grants' eighteen-foot inboard Lyman wooden boat all the way from Parry Sound to Sans Souci, memorizing every rock, channel, and buoy along the forty-five-minute trip. I even knew how to change a shear pin for the inevitable times when Tori and I hit something while driving the smaller ten-horsepower outboard.

Being in a boat on the bay with Tori was pure freedom. With the wind in my face and my hair blowing, the faint smell of gasoline was intoxicating as we traversed the choppy blue water. I was a mariner relishing the open air and adventure. This felt more like a religious experience than any temple I had been in.

When I outgrew camp, I started spending long periods of time in the summer at Tori's cottage. Tori and I were the best of friends and I loved being with her. She was my confidante, my bosom buddy. We were like Anne of Green Gables and her friend Diana. I shared everything with her. The summer before I entered high school, I went for a full month. Daddy, wanting to acknowledge the Grants' hospitality, decided to purchase a gift for them. He was cheap, so when he said he was going to get them a canoe, I was thrilled beyond belief. What an extravagant gift! I had seen beautiful wooden canoes out on the bay, painted either red or forest green, traversing the water when it was calm, usually at early morning or dusk.

The canoe was delivered by Sears shortly before Daddy was going to take me up to Tori's. "I didn't know you could get canoes from Sears," I said in anticipation as the truck pulled into our driveway.

"Yes, and I got a really good deal on it. It was on sale," said Daddy predictably.

The driver in a grey one-piece uniform opened the back doors of the van and I watched the bow of the canoe emerge with the words "Indian Chief" emblazoned on the front, along with an image of a man with a full headdress on. While I didn't have the words or knowledge to fully identify this as a colonial characterization, it made me feel queasy inside. The canoe was made of foam and decorated with a textured birchbark look.

"We can't give this to the Grants. This isn't a canoe!" I yelled.

"What do you mean?" said my dad. "This is a great canoe. It's nice because it's so light and portable, not like those heavy wooden ones."

I was mortified and pleaded with him to take it back. He was adamant about keeping it and I hung my head in shame when he gifted it to the Grants with such pride.

When we got off the water taxi that took us to the island, Daddy lifted the lightweight boat over his head to deposit it on the dock. I watched Tori and her parents' faces while they received this floating mockery of a canoe. I couldn't detect any evidence of disgust.

Tori and I used the canoe over the summer, but it was hard to paddle. The thing was so light it sat high on the water, spinning around, making it impossible to steer. The Grants thanked my dad profusely, but when I went to their cottage the following summer, I noticed the "Indian Chief" canoe had left port.

There were two more things that would be lost in Georgian Bay: my glasses and my virginity.

Chapter 37
Bay Boys

TORI'S MOM OFTEN SENT US TO GET MILK OR BREAD AT GARSIDE Marina, and we gladly went to the little convenience store that was a ten-minute boat ride away. We'd hang outside near the snack shop by the dock, licking our ice-cream cones, talking to the good-looking guys who pumped gas and worked at the marina. They were known as "bay boys," locals who had grown up on Georgian Bay and lived in Parry Sound in the winter. They weren't boys at all. They were men – with jobs, boats, and facial hair. They all stayed in the bunkhouses up on the hill behind the marina. These were rough-hewn plywood cabins that had bunk beds, small kitchenettes, and not much else. There was no plumbing; an outhouse was tucked away into the trees for privacy.

The bay boys started inviting us to their evening parties at the bunkhouses, long after the marina had closed, and we happily accepted.

"Which one do you like?" Tori asked late one night while we were debriefing after a bunkhouse party, each of us tucked into our single bed in her cozy bedroom at the back of the cottage.

"I like Karl," I sighed.

Karl was a tall, lanky guy with straight dirty-blond hair who moved his whole head with a sideways jerk to displace the long bangs that constantly hung in his eyes. He had a quiet confidence about him that reminded me of Lawrence – who I still liked – but, hey, this was summer.

"You?" I bounced back to Tori.

"Gerry is cool. I really like him." Gerry looked a little like the musician Cat Stevens, whose songs "Wild World" and "Tea for the Tillerman" we knew line by line. We had also been to Massey Hall and seen Cat Stevens in concert. With his curly dark hair, moustache, and bearded face, Gerry had a charming manner about him, and he seemed a little more urban than the other rural bay boys.

The bunkhouse parties graduated to late-night revelries on the bay. Sometimes we all met on an uninhabited island to party or went to a designated gathering spot in the middle of Georgian Bay. With all the different vessels tied up ten to fifteen abreast, you had to climb over each gunwale to make your way down the long line of boats, sharing a beer or a toke as you went. This was the best. The black night sky illuminated only by stars – or if we were lucky a full moon – met at the horizon with silhouettes of evergreens as far as your eye could see. We were like castaways, the sound of water lapping against the hulls of the boats our constant refrain. The hash and pot we smoked helped to maintain the illusion.

Somehow the Grants trusted us. When we escaped each night, Tori's Dad would simply say, "Remember to take a flashlight and extra shear pins, just in case." We would come home in the middle of the night, stoned on hash, giggling and trying to whisper as we tied up the fourteen-foot cedar-strip outboard. It was on one of these nights that I lost my glasses.

Tori, manoeuvring the Johnson outboard motor, was coming in to dock. My job was to jump out at the perfect time, with rope in hand, to tie up the boat. I guess I got my timing a little off, or the wind came up, or I was just too darn high, but whatever the case, I jumped and planted my left foot firmly on the dock but my right was still in the boat. The engine was off but the boat began drifting away from the dock. My legs were splitting wider and wider. How far apart could they go before I'd fall in? Tori was laughing uncontrollably and was desperately trying to stifle it so as not to wake her parents.

"Tori, Tori, help," I whispered in a panic. I could see the hilarity in the situation and went back and forth between laughter and dread. I had to pick a side to commit to – dock or boat – or end up in the cold dark water. I hurled myself onto the dock, barely making it, and lost my glasses in the leap. The next day we donned goggles, dived deep in the water near the rock crib of the dock, but to no avail. My glasses were gone forever.

I still had a few weeks left at the cottage before I was due to go home and it was extremely challenging to navigate life without being able to see. Everything was just one big blur. When we had island parties, I asked someone who wore glasses if I could borrow them just for a few minutes to get my bearings as I scrambled around rocks to get the lay of the land.

One night, Tori and I scored an evening alone with Karl and Gerry at the bunkhouse. We had discovered that our attraction for these boys was reciprocated. I was on the top bunk making out with Karl, and Tori was on the bottom with Gerry. Karl got up to use the outhouse and I rolled over to talk to Tori and Gerry, but without glasses I had no depth perception, so I fell right off the bed slamming onto the floor, sending sparks flying from the little electric heater. I was so embarrassed I pretended I had passed out. The only thing that was hurt was my ego.

Tori and I decided that this was the summer we were going to lose our virginity. We were both interested in demystifying the experience. Rather than waiting for it be a naturally romantic occurrence, we had discussed the value of taking the initiative and just getting on with it, to discover what all the fuss was about. While I liked Karl, I wanted to have sex with someone I wasn't attached to. Literally an in-and-out-experience. I chose Nedley, a very good-looking guy with a charismatic appeal who had worked at the marina for years. He was always flirting with Tori and me. He was several years our senior and it seemed like he toyed with every woman he met, so my thinking was that if I encouraged him, he would succumb – like a moth to a candle.

Nedley didn't know I was a virgin – or maybe he did – but one night, when we were at a party at the marina, I ventured off to visit him in his solo bunkhouse. I guess because of his age and seniority he had earned his own private quarters.

The experience was fleeting and disappointing. It was not at all what I imagined it would be, and as Nedley snored after our brief encounter, I went back to the party to head home with Tori. I untied the boat from the dock, climbed in, sitting down on the hard-wooden bench, a little gingerly.

"What's up with you? Are you okay?" asked Tori.

"Yup." I smirked. There wasn't much I could keep from Tori. "You know how we said we were going to lose our virginity this summer? Well –I just lost mine – to Nedley."

Tori shook her head and began to chuckle as she pulled hard on the cord to start the motor.

"What? What's so funny?"

"Well, I lost my virginity last night with – Nedley."

Like I said, I shared everything with Tori.

Chapter 38
Hippie High

THE THOUGHT OF STARTING HIGH SCHOOL WITHOUT MY GLASSES was daunting. I wanted to wait until my prescription was ready, but they were going to take a while, so I borrowed Daddy's thick black square frames to manoeuvre my way through the halls of York Mills High School. I was way too embarrassed to actually wear them, so I'd go up to a classroom door, remove the glasses from my pocket, and quickly put them on to find out what the room number was. It was a painful, slow process and I was late for every class the first few days. I suffered and sat at the front of the room, so no one could see me. It was *not* how I wanted to begin this rite of passage.

My pool of friends became wider and my consumption of hash regular. They seemed to go together. At lunch, a group of us – the "stoner" crowd – passed a pipe of hash around, in an inconspicuous spot, on the grassy hill behind the school, and then went back to class. I was a good student: quiet, polite, and I did my work diligently. No teacher ever suspected that I smoked drugs. I earned high grades in most subjects – although math and science always eluded me – because I figured out what teachers wanted and gave it back to them. It seemed so simple. I wondered why my friends couldn't figure this out. I found synonyms to reflect the words the teachers used to describe their assignments, embedding them in my work. I listened carefully to what they said they wanted, and then regurgitated this back to them like a bird feeding her hatchlings.

English class was where I could be creative, become absorbed in the novels we read, and find my own literary voice. I wrote short stories and poetry, sometimes putting my lyrics to music on the piano. It was in writing that I unleashed my conflicting emotions of wonder, loss, disdain, love and hate.

I was challenging power and society's expectations, and questioning the choices adults made to live such structured boring lives – working nine to five to pay the bills. The monotony and routine seemed stifling to me. I wanted more, something different, more creative, unique, dynamic. I wanted to challenge the status quo.

I remember sitting on the floor in the den: the record player blasting *Piano Man* by Billy Joel, the house full of friends, singing all the lyrics, while fumes of hash permeated the air – and in those moments, I felt connection, joy, and freedom. This is how we were meant to live. I had an open door – all were welcome. 77 Plymbridge was social headquarters. Word got out when my father was out of town – this was before the Internet – and different cliques from high school came: the jocks, the stoners, most were people I knew, some I didn't.

"Who's that guy in the tennis outfit?" I asked Lawrence one night at one of my parties.

"Don't know, never seen him before. Why the tennis togs?" said Lawrence, the antithesis of a jock, as he slowly exhaled the smoke of his perfectly rolled joint.

The first time I got stoned, I was with Lawrence. I didn't realize that you don't get high right away when you smoke pot or hash. It takes a few times. We were at my house, using knives we had heated on the stove. The process involved putting the hash onto the hot knives and then inhaling the pungent smoke with a straw.

"I don't feel anything, do you?" I asked Lawrence.

"No, not yet."

"What will it feel like? How will I know?"

"Ohh, you'll just know when you're high."

Lawrence was using the straw to inhale the thin line of smoke when suddenly the small piece of tar-like black hash got sucked up onto the end of the straw like a spitball that had failed to launch.

I broke out into uncontrollable laughter. The kind of laughter I couldn't stop, where no sound was actually coming out of my mouth and I couldn't breathe. My stomach was beginning to hurt, but hilarity took precedence over pain. Lawrence was killing himself laughing too, low gasps of his breath punctuating the air.

"We're definitely high now, Marsh."

I was reckless in my partying, defying Daddy and his possessions. He had a brass hookah pipe that he'd purchased on one of his travels to India. It was proudly displayed on a shelf in the den, with all his other pipes, and was never meant to be used. I pulled it down at one of my parties, filled the pipe base with water, and added pot to the container – meant only for tobacco – passed it around, and we sucked, two at a time, on the long hoses that were delicately wrapped in green thread.

One night, someone yelled, "There's a fire in the den!" I went running to find the orange swivel-chair cushion on fire – someone had dropped a cigarette down the seam. I put out the fire and turned the cushion upside down so Daddy wouldn't see the huge burn-hole.

Several days later, Daddy called me into the kitchen, "How did that chair in the den get burned?"

"I don't know."

He sighed in exasperation, knowing full well that I was responsible for the singed cushion.

Even when Daddy was just out for the evening, I had parties. He would come home to find the house filled with my friends, most of whom he'd never met before.

"What's going on here, Marsha. I didn't give you permission to have a party and what is that smell?"

"It's American cigarettes, Dad."

I looked at my dad with disgust and disdain. He wanted things a certain way – his way – and I felt stifled. *His mind is like a tunnel, with his, the only train passing through,* I wrote in my diary. I was living to the lyrics of the music I carried in my head: Bob Dylan, Joni Mitchell, James Taylor.

I read *Don't Push the River: It Flows by Itself* by Gestalt therapist Barry Stevens and she spoke to me in a profound way. Stevens inspired me to seize each of life's moments and engage in them fully. The very title was a mantra for both Tori and I to let life unfold, be spontaneous, find your true self. I stopped wearing a bra, removed the seams from my blue jean overalls to fashion a long flowing dress, grew my hair long past my shoulders, and embraced life as a free spirit.

Daddy didn't know what to do with me.

Chapter 39
Tomcats

WHILE I CAME UNDONE, DADDY STARTED TO MATURE. HE BEGAN dating a Jewish woman his own age, Ellen Cohen. Actually, he alternated his time between Ellen and Gwen.

Gwen had come into our family as one of the young pregnant women my mother had hired. She was originally from Australia and my father liked to tease her when she used colloquialisms from Down Under. I was too young to know the story of why Gwen came to Canada, or what happened to her baby. Gwen was just part of our family. She ate with us, came with us on family outings, and always just seemed to be around, both before my mother died and after.

I admired Gwen. She worked in an office and had her own apartment – a one-bedroom in a low-rise building. I loved going to visit her on my own, listening to records from her vast collection, or going out for lunch with her, which seemed so glamorous. She was like the strong independent women I watched on TV – Mary Tyler Moore and Julia, who had careers of their own and didn't seem to need or depend on men. Gwen was like a parent figure, I could count on her, but she acted more like a friend. When I had pressed Daddy for money to get my expensive perm done, it turned out to cost even more than I'd thought. I couldn't possibly ask Daddy for additional money, so I went to Gwen and she was happy to help me out. Daddy used to say, "Gwen is a good sport." She didn't wear makeup, was athletic

– often skiing with us at Collingwood on the weekends – and had a no-nonsense approach to life. If Daddy wanted someone to watch TV with him on a Saturday night, she came over on short notice. Daddy didn't have to impress Gwen. He could sit in the den farting, while watching TV in his striped bathrobe – the one I called Jacob's coat of many colours – and Gwen didn't judge, but just seemed content to be with him. Gwen had been through so much with our family. She watched from the sidelines, while Daddy married two different women, after Mommy died. I think she thought her time had come, and the comfort and ease they shared would eventually progress to marriage. This was not to be.

Daddy's time with Ellen Cohen involved a little more work. She, too, came over for meals, but Daddy put more effort into what he was wearing and cooking: preparing fancy dishes like paella or pheasant under glass (minus the glass), the pheasant being one he had shot on one of his hunting expeditions.

Ellen slept over, but Daddy lied and told me, when I woke up in the morning, that she had just arrived. I knew she had slept over because I had seen where she'd attempted to hide her car. Late at night after a party, when Tori and I got a ride home from a friend, I'd often say, "Drop Tori off before me," so we'd pass my house to go to Green Valley and then turn around. There, at the end of the road, was Ellen's red Toyota, standing out like a stop sign.

When I got up in the morning, Daddy said, "Look who just dropped in for breakfast." One time I noticed that Ellen was wearing the same top she had on the night before – and it was inside out.

Ellen had two children who were close to my age: a boy and a girl. The boy was a year older than me, and the girl was my age, but they seemed like they were from a different planet. They were what you called nerdy kids. They both had pallid complexions, making them look ghoulish, like they lived underground. They were shy, non-communicative teens who spent more time reading printed words than speaking them.

"Marsha, Ellen's kids are coming over tonight for dinner and I want you to make an effort to talk to them, spend some time with them."

"They don't even talk! I'm not spending time with those creepy kids." Despite my protests, I had to hang out with them.

Ellen was crazy about my dad and fluttered around, trying to please him. She was as animated as her kids were quiet, filling the house with chatter about mindless things that my dad often tuned out. They both belonged to Temple Emmanuel – I suppose that's where they met – and I wasn't sure what Daddy saw in her. Maybe he was at a point where sex was not his primary driver and he wanted some admiration and companionship. But why not choose Gwen?

Ellen was okay-looking but wasn't like the typical sex kittens Daddy had brought home or married. Her thin black hair – teased on the top to give it body – hung loosely to her shoulders. She had a kind, open face, with a genuine smile. I didn't mind Ellen. I felt a little sorry for her. She seemed so earnest, always trying so hard with my dad and me. It must have been challenging to have such quiet kids when she was such a talkative person. When she asked me if I wanted a summer job as a typist in the office she worked in, I thought, Why not? I had good typing skills – must have been from playing piano – and this saved me from having to job hunt. Also, she said she could drive me to and from work. It seemed like a good deal. As it turned out, the hardest part was the car ride there and back every day. She talked non-stop and it was more exhausting being with her in the car than doing the actual job. Then, if she stayed for dinner at the end of the day, I suffered from an excess of Ellen.

I was glad I could escape and spend time with my own love interest – Lawrence – who knew how to enjoy the quiet. Lawrence and I would put on a Neil Young album – *Harvest Moon* was our favourite – and we simply listened to the lyrics, without talking at all. When we did talk, we had long, meaningful conversations about life – often for hours on the telephone – when we got home after school. It seemed like we had our most intimate conversations on the phone. When we were alone, face to face, it was harder to speak about the depth of our feelings. I loved him, or at least I think I did. I had never really felt that kind of love before. I got that butterfly feeling in the pit of my stomach whenever I saw Lawrence and wanted to be with him as much as possible. He was, however, a little inaccessible. He wasn't the type of guy who wanted to be tied down to a "girlfriend." There was a reason everyone called him "the cat" – affection and attention were on his terms. He was cool, a little detached, and valued his independence. It was what I liked about him, yet I wanted more. I aspired to live the hippie lifestyle – free love, without strings – but I was fighting my own internal desire to love and be loved by only one boy. And that boy was Lawrence.

It was Julie who broke the news that Lawrence was leaving. He was quitting school and going to live out west in B.C. with their older brother, Allan. I was devastated. I did understand his need to leave. I knew he felt isolated, alienated, and saw no purpose in school and wanted a different kind of life. I had never told Lawrence how I felt about him. I was scared and really didn't know how to articulate my feelings. Also, I enjoyed what we had. What if my declaration of love scared him away? We hadn't kissed or been physically intimate and now any chance we had of moving forward was gone. That familiar feeling of losing love re-emerged.

Lawrence was traveling to Vancouver in a van with his friend Martin and said he would come to say goodbye the night before he was set to leave. I yearned, prayed – even though I didn't believe in God – that he would come. I wrote him a poem, as a way to share my unexpressed love.

It got very late and I started to give up hope that Lawrence was coming when I heard a light knock on the front door. I let him in and we quietly slipped upstairs to my bedroom, not wanting to wake Daddy. We sat on the edge of my bed. There was so much I wanted to say, yet the thoughts in my head couldn't move down to materialize from my mouth. I wanted to reach out and touch him but was terrified of making any sudden movement. I might never see him again. Shouldn't I just be bold and say something, do something to let him know how I felt? What did I have to lose? What if he didn't feel the way I did? Every part of my body was longing to grab him, hold on to him tight for dear life, like a baby chimp to its mother.

The room was pitch-black, too dark to see, which gave me some comfort in a tiny cavity in the pit of my chest. "Let's lie down," he said and my body dutifully responded. We lay fully clothed, our bodies aligned face to face, taking up a fraction of space on my antique brass bed. Bob Dylan's lyrics "Lay, lady, lay. Lay upon my big brass bed" popped into my head. My breath was quick, rising and falling in both desire and apprehension. This was all so new to me. I inhaled his scent: cigarettes and a musky earthy aroma like autumn leaves in the woods. His hand caressed my arm and I felt the warm pads of his fingers even through my denim shirt. When his hand reached mine, he explored each of my fingers, one by one. It was as if my hand wasn't attached to me, or it belonged to someone else. I became that hand. All my bodily sensations were centred there. The rest of me had floated off somewhere else. He clasped my hand within his tightly. We pressed our hands together as we kissed. My lips seemed to know what to do and moved on their own, yet in sync with his. I had no brain, no thoughts, no body – only lips and hands connecting. Slowly, I felt our arms, with hands still clasped, moving from our thighs to up, up, above our heads. My hand and arm rose, following his without effort. We were now one arm and one leg, stretched taut together on our sides. I melted into him like wax from a candle.

Blood began rushing into my head. My arm was starting to tingle, lifted above my head like that for so long. My brain was back. I'm loving this, but how to get our arms back down to our sides? If I move my arm, will he let go? I don't want to let go of his clasped hand, but my arm is pounding. It's all I can think about. With hands still clasped, heart palpitating, I initiated a slow, gentle movement of our arms back down to our thighs. It was fluid and effortless and we stayed connected. Crisis averted.

There was something about our clasped hands that felt so intimate to me, even more than our kissing. What was it? The tight grip and being held was comforting, loving, and gentle. I felt grounded in a kind of love and touch that I had never experienced before. I felt safe.

Lawrence stayed all night. We didn't progress further than kissing and never took our clothes off. We didn't need to. We expressed our love in such a tender, pure way. I felt joy, passion, and affirmation, that we shared the same deep feelings. I sent him off with my poem:

> *You came into my life as a stray*
> *And now you tell you're leaving that way*
> *You slid through the back porch door*
> *Settled down, and asked for no more*
> *I fed you, I loved you, I cared each day*
> *Our friendship blossomed in more than one way*
> *There were times I was doubtful I wanted a pet*
> *Now the doubts have all vanished and I'm thankful we met*
> *The woman is right when she sings in her song*
> *"You don't know what you've got till it's gone"*
> *There are things that I wish I'd said before*
> *But it seems now, there's no time anymore*

Chapter 40
Working World

IN THE EVENINGS I SOMETIMES BABYSAT FOR FAMILIES IN THE valley, but I wanted a more regular after-school job, so I was pleased when I was hired as a part-time employee at Shoppers Drug Mart. I worked every day after school in the underbelly of the drugstore. Void of fluorescent lighting, I toiled in the dark cramped basement unpacking boxes, wielding a tagging gun to stick price tags onto every single product. It was a job predominately staffed by boys from my school, who were a little older than me. The pinups of naked women strategically placed in our sightlines annoyed me, but as the lone female voice, my remarks on how this was offensive had little impact.

The girls worked upstairs on cash, but I preferred not having to deal with the public. I got panicky at the thought of having to use the cash register. My previous job, selling popcorn at the Fairlawn Theatre, had proved to be a disaster when I failed miserably at trying to calculate the proper change. Customers grew impatient and yelled at me, or asked, "What's the matter, can't you subtract?" Well, no I couldn't, not without using my fingers, and it was extremely stressful.

Once on a crowded evening when the movie *Jaws* was playing, the lineup to get popcorn had dissolved into a horde of people, making it difficult to tell who was there first. A guy who I guess had been waiting a long time bellowed, "What's the matter, am I black or something. Why aren't you serving me?"

I lost it and told him, "With that racist attitude, you aren't going to be served at all." I had to agree with my supervisor when she told me that I wasn't cut out for customer service.

The job at Shoppers was painfully mundane and boring. The only pleasure I could find was laughing with my co-workers at our supervisor, Frank. Frank was a tall guy with a crew cut who always dressed the same: a short-sleeved white shirt, with a visible undershirt, all tucked into grey pants that he constantly hiked up, even though his large belly seemed to keep everything in place. Frank had found a way to have a full-time job without actually doing any work. He sat in his little office at the back of the basement, the newspaper spread open on his desk, picking his nose while he read. We often tried to catch him in the act, sneaking up to his office to ask him something, timing it to when his finger would be buried knuckle-deep.

While I hated the job, I loved the money. I didn't have to ask Daddy for cash, which involved a fight, as he always interrogated me about what I was buying and why I needed it. I could purchase hash and still put money aside. I was toying with the idea of moving out. Lawrence had done it. His letters shared all his adventures: how much he was enjoying working and was looking forward to renting his own apartment. I detested living at home and thought perhaps if I saved enough, I, too, could live on my own, or move out with Tori.

The job at Shoppers was only during the school year, so when Tori said we could both get a job in the summer at Garside Marina, working in the snack shop, I was thrilled. We could stay at her cottage, earn good money, and have a rich social life with the bay boys. I thought Daddy would also be relieved to have me gone all summer.

I was seventeen years old, entering grade eleven in the fall. I didn't know it at the time, but my wish to move out, leave home, and never *have* to live under my father's roof again was going to come true. Careful what you wish for.

Chapter 41
Love, Dreams, and Delusions

I LOVED LAWRENCE, YET I KNEW HE WASN'T BOYFRIEND MATERIAL. While painful, his leaving helped me to move on and accept this fact. I wanted more of a commitment. I'd had a taste of love and it was delicious.

Gary and I had known each other since junior high. We moved in the same circle of friends and he was at my parties at 77 Plymbridge. Gary was part of the jock crowd: he played football and was on all the school's sport teams. He played a lead part in the school production of *Guys and Dolls* and was comfortable on centre stage. He was very different from Lawrence: more canine, less cat. Actually, he was very different from me. My musical tastes ranged from folk to Motown: Joni Mitchell, Stevie Wonder. He was into rock and roll and heavy metal: the Rolling Stones and Led Zeppelin. I was a stoner. He was a drinker. I was contemplative and calm. He was funny and restless. There was a directness, a scrappiness, he had that was appealing. You knew when Gary entered the room. His booming voice and wit created an energy that was charismatic.

While Gary was good-looking, with his hazel boudoir eyes and brown shaggy hair, it wasn't his looks alone that drew me to him. It seemed like he was an underdog, blamed or accused for things that I knew he didn't do. If we were at a party and the music was turned up too loud, someone would point to him, "Gary, turn that music down, we don't want the cops to come." I felt bad for him, but it was more than that. People misunderstood him. He revealed deep, thoughtful, and sensitive feelings, which I could relate to. Also, he was not one of the rich kids. He came from a working-class family; his parents had emigrated from Britain, and he lived far from the valley, in a small house that backed onto the 401 highway. He was the kind of guy who could commit.

When the warm days of June came, signalling the end of the school year, Tori and I left for the summer jobs we had secured on Georgian Bay. I was reluctant to leave Gary. We had spent a lot of time together hanging out at my house on weekends and after school. Gary had now replaced Lawrence, taking his throne in the orange upholstered swivel chair in the den. Gary said he'd come and visit me up north, but the logistics of getting there by bus and trying to coordinate a boat ride to the island made it seem unlikely. We both promised we would write.

It seems incredible, that at seventeen years old, Tori and I were the ones to run the marina snack shop. We worked a full-time shift, opening and closing at the same time each day. The little "restaurant" sold twelve flavours of hand-scooped ice cream, cigarettes, candies, and other small food items. We also prepared coffee, grilled cheese sandwiches, soup (Campbells, from a can), and hotdogs. We plugged in the hotdog machine first thing in the morning, loading up a dozen foot-longs onto the stainless-steel rollers, where they would rotate non-stop all day like a Ferris wheel. While the pungent, savoury smell was appealing, they were so dried up by the time patrons came in for lunch, it was hard not to stifle a laugh when an unsuspecting customer would inquire, "Those hot dogs fresh?"

"Oh yeah, fresh and juicy."

Mostly, people came in wanting ice-cream cones. If there was a lineup, scooping from the frozen bins in the freezer was a cold job that caused my forearm and hand to throb with numbness.

We got to hang out with the bay boys, who we knew quite well by now. During the lull, when boats weren't lined up for gas, the boys came into the snack shop to smoke cigarettes, drink coffee, and chat with us.

At night we were partying, either out on the bay or back at the marina in one of the bunkhouses. Nedley was still around – he was a lifer. Any memory he had of deflowering Tori and me wasn't evident, and we settled back into our friendly teasing. Nedley introduced us to his brother, Neil, who was also working at the marina. He was older, married with a young baby, but was the image of a stereotypical hippie. He had light brown, shoulder-length curly hair and wore a dark leather string around his neck that had a brightly coloured goulimine bead hanging from the end of it. He even drove a beat-up bright yellow Volkswagen van, which we saw parked at the Glenn Burney Marina when we went to town to go grocery shopping with Tori's mom.

Neil knew things. He, too, had read Barry Stevens's *Don't Push the River*, and we had deep discussions about how to be your best self and live free, in the moment, without falling into the trappings of a life that society expected of you. I questioned him about how he could do this with a wife and baby. He said they had a non-traditional relationship, and were free to love and be with whoever they chose. Neil was inquisitive, asking Tori and me thoughtful questions to help us uncover our values and beliefs about life. We got high together and were drawn to Neil's dreams for the future. He wanted to move out west to B.C. and start his own carpentry business. He was talented, able to build cabinets and furniture. He had even come up with his own unique design for the hull of a sailboat. His plan was to build a boat and then sail it to Malta. He didn't only build things out of wood, he also built up Tori and me to feel special, smart, and capable. In his eyes, we were young women who could achieve whatever we set our sights on. He was so much older than any other guy I'd met. His knowledge and confidence were intoxicating. We became enamoured with Neil; Tori slightly more so. Neil liked me as a friend, but I could see he was falling for Tori, and she for him.

Gary and I had kept our promise of writing to each other and exchanged letters over the summer. While I missed him, I also was having a really good time being free and hanging out with so many different people; older guys, especially Neil. I went in and out of loving Gary and loving my freedom.

Gary surprised me with a visit to Georgian Bay. I was shocked that he had made such an effort to come and see me. I was excited to see him, yet when he arrived I felt conflicted. He seemed so much younger than the "men" we were hanging out with. The bay boys had a maturity and confidence in how they carried themselves. Gary's arrival pointed out the disparity between the city boy and the country boys. Gary, who was confident in his own environment, was like a duck out of water on Georgian Bay. I didn't treat him well. I laughed too loud, flirted too much with Neil, Nedley, and the other guys to show off my new independent life. He was as perplexed by my behaviour as I was confused. I seemed to love him more when he wasn't around, enchanted by the idea of him. I wanted commitment, yet I didn't want to be tied down. I felt badly about how I treated him but was relieved when he left.

Shortly after his visit, a letter arrived from Gary that freaked me out. He declared his love for me, in a profound, emotional, and vulnerable way. While it stirred up pleasure, it also caused discomfort. No one had ever professed their love for me so directly. He was so serious: about me, our relationship, and wanting to commit to something more, bigger. I wasn't sure what to do with it. After days of deliberation, I wrote him back on Garside Marina stationary.

> *Dear Gary,*
>
> *Well, where do I start? First of all, you must realize that it is very difficult for me to express my feelings on paper. I would much rather be able to talk to you, but it isn't possible at this moment, so a letter must suffice. I had no idea that you felt <u>so strongly</u>. It upset me a bit to discover that you are*

so serious. I suppose you could say it scared me more than upset me.

It's scary to find out that someone loves you, because along with that love comes dependence, ties and expectations. I love you Gary. You're a special person and I care for you. But I don't really know if I'm in love with you and there is a difference between loving and being in love. It's hard to make it definite because my feelings are not constant. They change every day. There are days when I am in love with you and then there are the days when I don't want to see you. Do you see what I mean? I really think you fell for the wrong person. I just can't get really serious, that's all. One of my problems is that I am in love with love. Everywhere you go in our society, someone is promoting love. It's on TV, the radio, everywhere. So, I fantasize about love a lot. When I'm away from you, I think about you quite often and then I start to fantasize, because I'm not really thinking of you, but some super human being who simply doesn't exist. What I'm trying to say is that when it comes to love, I live in a fantasy world. I picture love as something that it isn't. Obviously, it tends to fuck me up a bit.

As for you Gary, if everything is really loose, we will have a cool time. Sometimes I wonder how we ever met, since we really are so different.

Well, I shall sign off now, because I am working and there are certain things that need doing. Tori and I are going fishing tonight with these guys we met who are from Pennsylvania. They are really neat guys. It's so rough out, so it should be quite an experience!!

I hope things are a bit clearer for you now. Be happy Gary! This world of ours is a pretty neat place.

Take care!

Love Marsha

It was as clear as the murky bottom of the bay we careened over every day.

The one person who I thought knew the true path forward was Neil. He had a wisdom and knowledge I valued, which would help me move forward with my dream of moving out of the confines of my father's home. Neil also had come up with a concrete plan on how to do it. Tori and I were going to move out west to B.C. with him. He could support the two of us with his carpentry work, if we wanted to finish high school, or we could get a job. Disillusioned with school, I thought this would give me a clean break. What was the point in going to school when I was learning absolutely nothing? It was the middle of summer, we still had another month to go in our jobs at the marina, but we told the owners on Friday that we were leaving the next day and would not be back to work on Monday. Tori announced our plan to her parents that night after dinner, while we washed the dishes. They had company for dinner, so their pleading had a quality of restraint to it. While Tori brushed her teeth, preparing for bed, I could hear her mom standing outside the bathroom door, distraught, begging her not to do this.

We were both so confident, so sure, that what we were doing was the right thing, what we were meant to do. The adults in our world simply didn't understand us.

I lay awake in bed, eager for the adventure I was about to embark on. The life I had been reading about, dreaming of, and wishing for was coming true. I took the words of Fritz Perls, the found of Gestalt therapy, to heart:

"I am not in this world to live up to other people's expectations, nor do I feel that the world must live up to mine."

Chapter 42
Shock and Awe

NEIL, TORI, AND I LEFT IN THE MORNING TO MAKE THE THREE-hour drive from Parry Sound to Toronto. Our plan was for Tori and me to pack up our clothes, take money out of our bank accounts, and say goodbye to a few friends. I especially wanted to connect with Gary to tell him I was leaving.

Neil dropped me off at home first and then went with Tori to her house so she could pack her stuff. He said he'd be back in about an hour or so. I had time to do some laundry and to tell Daddy I was leaving. Two dirty jobs. Daddy and Ellen were both home. When I walked in, they were in the kitchen getting ready to sit down to lunch. An assortment of salami, cheese, bagels, and dill pickles was attractively arranged on a wooden platter on the kitchen table. The smell of fresh bagels brought recognition and comfort to my nose, but my stomach felt like I was at the top of a roller coaster, about to lose the contents of my intestines. While I had fantasized about the satisfaction I would feel in telling Daddy I was leaving, I hadn't considered exactly *what* I was going to say.

"You're home early from the cottage. Is everything okay?" said Daddy.

"Yes, everything is fine. Actually, it couldn't be better. I've made a decision to move out," I said in a tone of overconfidence. My fingers tightened into my palms. I could feel my nails digging into my skin.

My dad's tight-lipped mouth parted. "What do you mean? What about your job at the marina? Where are you moving to?"

"Daddy, you're never going to understand this. But for the first time in a long time, I have a plan, that feels right to me. I have never been so sure before. Tori and I are going to move to B.C. with Neil. He is super smart and talented." There, I had said it.

Silence. Ellen looked like she was watching a tennis game as she jerked her head back and forth looking from Daddy to me. I waited. Would he explode in anger or try to reason with me? I had my armour on, heavily defended for whatever was going to come my way.

"What about school?" Daddy asked.

Okay, he was going for the rational approach. "I may go to school, I don't know. I'll see when I get there. Neil can get a job as a carpenter – he's really skilled –and he can support both of us."

"Now, Marsha, I know we don't get along, but listen to me. You're making a big mistake here. Quitting school, going with this guy, Neil? Who is he? How long have you *even* known him? How old is he?"

Daddy's familiar belligerence and anger were kicking in. Rationality was in short supply. This fuelled me forward.

"Look, Dad, I'm not asking for your approval, your opinion, or even your money. I've made up my mind and that's that. I don't want to live here anymore!" I turned and left the room, not knowing where my feet would take me. I could hear my heart in my ears, like a stethoscope. I had no doubts at all, though – this was my time and I was going to seize it. I gathered up the dirty clothes I had brought back from the cottage and went down to the basement to throw in a load of laundry. As I was replaying the conversation in my head, feeling proud of my ability to stand up to my dad, I felt a presence behind me. I turned to see Ellen standing at the entrance to the laundry room, one raised hand holding on to the doorframe. Here we go, I thought. Daddy's sent his messenger to try to talk me out of it.

"Ellen, there's nothing you can say that can convince me to stay."

"No, I wasn't going to do that. There's something I want to give you."

She entered the room, came right up to me, pressing her mouth to my ear, and said in a whisper, "I think it's great what you're doing. You are only young once. It takes courage to follow your dreams." She then took a wad of folded money from her pocket and pressed the bills into my hands.

It was my turn to be shocked. "Ellen, I can't accept this."

"Just take it. It's our little secret. Please don't tell your dad."

Ellen left the room as quietly as she had entered it. I smiled, my admiration of Ellen going up a notch. I felt affirmed that yes, I was doing the right thing. Perhaps I had awakened in Ellen memories of opportunities she wished she'd taken when she was young. Or maybe she just wanted me out of the picture so Daddy could have peace and she could have him all to herself. Whatever the case, I counted the bills and gratefully tucked them into the side pocket of my blue jeans.

Chapter 43
Taking Flight

I heard the phone ring. "Marsha, Tori's father is calling from a telephone booth in Parry Sound. He wants to talk to her," Daddy yelled out while I was carrying my bag downstairs to put in Neil's van. I went outside to tell Tori, who was in the driveway, waiting with Neil.

"Marsh, I have to talk to him. I can't leave without a proper goodbye."

"Okay, Neil and I will stay outside. Don't be too long. We *have* to leave before my dad thinks up some crazy way to stop us. I don't trust him."

Neil and I waited for what seemed like an interminable amount of time. I felt like a heroine in one of those science-fiction movies, trying to get away from the monster but one of my limbs was trapped. Time is running out, hurry, hurry, pull your leg out, here he comes!

Finally, Tori emerged from the front door. She walked over to where we were standing by the van. Her face had that worried anxious look I had seen before, whenever she had to deal with any kind of confrontation. Daddy was hovering on the front patio, door ajar.

"Look, guys, I had a long talk with my dad. He pleaded with me, begged me even, not to go until I talk to him face to face. My parents are leaving the cottage tomorrow to come down to the city. Can we just wait one day?"

I let out a sigh. My limb was free, but the monster still loomed.

"Sure, there's no real rush. We have a month to get out west, what's one more day?" Neil, said, the sound of reason in his voice.

"Well, we can't stay together here at my house. What about your place, Tori? Nobody's home," I said.

"No way, I don't want to stay there. I don't know exactly what time my parents will be home and I don't want to risk them walking in on us."

"Let's just get in the van and we can find somewhere to park overnight. I have sleeping bags and pillows. We can pick up some food on the way" said Neil.

"Perfect. Let's go." I could see Daddy approaching. Before he could get too close, I yelled out, "Goodbye, Daddy! We're off." I wasn't sure if he had talked to Mr. Grant on the phone, or heard Tori talking, and knew we were going to wait an extra day. But even if he had, he didn't know where we going. *We* didn't even know. We got into the van and drove out of the valley to find a park. Tori was in the passenger seat, beside Neil. I was relieved to be in the back, the bumpy ride – those bad shocks Neil had talked about – jostling me in my seat, affirming our escape.

I now had time to tell Gary in person that we were leaving, so I called him later from a payphone, asking if he could come meet us at the local park where we had camped out for the night. He was going to call a few other friends and we could hang out together.

It was a beautiful warm August evening. We were sitting in the park covered in a green leafy canopy of trees, which helped, somewhat, to provide camouflage for Neil's bright yellow van. The evening sound of crickets and tree frogs had replaced the cicadas that hummed so loudly during the day. When I saw Gary, his good friend Tom, and my childhood friend Leigh come walking up the path, I felt a rush of comfort to see familiar faces. I was grateful that they made the effort to seek us out.

Gary had met Neil during his visit to Georgian Bay. They shook hands and we introduced Leigh and Tom to Neil. We assembled on the grass with Neil and Tori sitting on the running board of the van, identifying by their close physical proximity that they were a couple. Neil pulled out a plastic bag of pot, and while he rolled a joint Tori and I shared our plans for our impending journey to Vancouver. If Gary was upset, angry, or confused, he didn't show it. Neither Leigh nor Tom registered any emotion on their faces either. I didn't feel judged, but their barrage of questions on the practicality of it all indicated silently they thought we were foolish "running away" from home with a man who was almost twice our age. "How long will the trip take?" Will you register for school there? Neil, have you been there before?" Leigh and Tom took turns firing questions at us. Neil didn't mention the wife and baby he was leaving behind. Neither did we.

The anxiety and stress I had felt during the day was washed away by the beer and the grass we consumed while listening to music on Neil's boom box. We talked, laughed, and shared stories. I relished the delight of wearing a sleeveless shirt on a warm summer evening. The Seals and Crofts song "Summer breeze, makes me feel fine, blowing through the jasmine of my mind" was a perfect backdrop to our setting

Tom was the first to notice the headlights. "A car is coming down the path!" he warned. An automobile approaching was unusual; it wasn't a path meant for cars. We had just driven the van down to park in an unobtrusive spot. "Shit, it's the cops!" Tom said.

Before we could register the significance of this – after all, we were high – two uniformed police officers were walking toward us, their yellow beam of light guiding the way. The bag of grass was sitting open on the floor of the van. Without speaking, Neil rolled up the bag and stashed it in a side opening in the van door. In one swift movement, Tom grabbed the bag from where Neil had hidden it and stuffed it down his pants, pulling out his plaid shirt to cover any apparent bulge. He moved like a gazelle in flight. He managed to do all this before the police were upon us.

"Hello, officers," Tom said as he took a puff on his Export cigarette. "What can we do for you?" If anyone could get away with being cool and confident, it was Tom. With his short-cropped hair, commanding voice, and ultra-conservative look, he could have passed for a cop himself.

"What are you doing here so late at night? Cars aren't allowed in this park," said one of the officers, while the other went to the back of the van to shine his flashlight on the licence plate.

"We're just enjoying a nice summer night, officer. There's no crime in that, is there? We'll move the car, sir," said Neil as he attempted to take control of the situation.

"Do you own this van?" the officer addressed Neil.

"Yes, it's mine."

"I'll need to see your licence. And we're going to have to search the van."

"Sure. I have nothing to hide. The van is a bit of a mess though, sorry about that. Is there something wrong, officer?"

The second officer who had been looking at the licence plate exchanged a glance with the cop who was doing all the talking. For the first time he spoke. He looked down at the small pad of paper he was holding and asked, "Is one of you girls Marsha Barrett?"

Abruptly, the high I had felt a minute ago vanished. I wasn't stoned anymore.

"Yes, that's me" I said, raising my hand, as if responding to an attendance roll call by a teacher.

The first cop was rifling through all the stuff in the van, clearly looking for something. When he stuck his hand deep into the pocket at the side of the van, there was no mistaking the tangible relief we all felt at the same time. Thank God Tom had acted so quickly.

I summoned up some courage. "Why do you have my name?" The police officer asked me to come with him and we walked to a clearing that was out of earshot of everyone else.

"Are you here under your own free will?"

"What do you mean? Yes, of course. These are my friends."

He took off his police cap, scratched his head, and looked me in the eye. "Your father is very worried about you. He said, this older fellow you're with – Neil, is his name, right? – has a plan to take you out of province. That true?"

"We have made a plan to go out west together to Vancouver, but it was my *own* decision to move there."

"How old are you?"

"Seventeen."

"You got some proof of your age? ID?"

"Yes, it's in the van. There is nothing illegal about deciding to move away from home."

"Well, maybe not, but you know, you *are* young to be moving so far away. You want to be careful about who you are partnering up with."

"How did you know to find me here at the park?"

"We got a call from your father. He reported that Neil had underage girls with him and was also involved in the use of illegal drugs. He gave us the licence plate number of the van. You ever use any drugs?"

"No," I lied.

The fear I had felt that the police would find something incriminating retreated, and rage took its place. How dare my father call the police and make up a story about Neil? He just thought he could use his power however he wanted to, not even considering my feelings or what I wanted. Hatred seeped through my body like an oozing wound.

The police didn't find anything in the van. With no evidence that we were breaking any law, they told us to remove the van from the park. We followed their orders.

Once in the van, we laughed with relief at the narrow escape we'd made, all of us talking over one another to tell our version of what we had felt in those moments, praising Tom for his quick reflex.

"How did the cops have my licence plate and your name?" Neil asked. I could feel the heat of shame and anger on my face as I described the lie my father had told the police.

"Well, thank goodness they didn't find the grass! I would have been charged for sure," said Neil.

We said a heartfelt goodbye to Leigh, Gary, and Tom and then Neil drove around looking for somewhere to park the van for the night. He found a larger park that had several paved spaces for cars. With his licence plate now known to the cops, we could run but we couldn't hide.

While Tori and Neil slept, I lay awake going over and over in my mind what Daddy had done. He seemed intent on stopping me and all I could feel was anger and frustration at his attempt to thwart my plans. The way he had done it was so deceitful. Lying to the police to tell them I was unwilling, when he knew full well I was desperate to move out of the house.

I wondered about tomorrow. I questioned whether Tori's resolve was as solid as mine. She wanted to move out west but didn't have the same strong hatred for her parents that I had for Daddy. She feared her father and had never really defied him.

I started to think about what I would do if Tori changed her mind. There was no turning back for me.

Chapter 44
Grounded

THE LIFE-SIZED BLACK-AND-WHITE PHOTOGRAPH OF THE NAKED couple was the proverbial writing on the wall. It hung across from the bed that Neil and I were sharing.

Tori's parents had convinced her not to go out west. Her dad used his contacts to get her a job as a counsellor at Camp Wapomeo – an all-girls camp in Algonquin Park – for the last month of the summer. That left me alone with Neil.

Daddy tried one more time to use the law to stop me. He wanted the cops to arrest Neil and charge him with "statutory rape." Those were the words he used. Daddy asked me to get an internal exam done at a doctor's office. There was no way I was going to do that. Besides, we hadn't even had sex, but I wasn't going to let Daddy know that. I saw my father one more time to tell him that Neil and I were delaying our trip out west until after the summer and in the meantime we were going to live together downtown.

"If you leave with that man, you will never step foot in this house again. Do you hear me? I will disown you."

I heard him. I would hear it in my head and wear it like an invisible cloak wherever I went.

Nobody would rent an apartment to Neil and me. He was a hippie and looked the part, with his shoulder-length hair, long fringed vest, and bell-bottom pants. He had no job, we weren't married, and we wanted a temporary apartment. One day when we were sitting on the curb beside his parked van on Brunswick Avenue, near College, contemplating another night sleeping in the van, Neil noticed a man and a woman – fellow hippies – in a driveway, packing band equipment into a truck. He went right up to them and started chatting. It turned out they were in a rock and roll band that was going on tour. Neil boldly asked if this was their house. They said they shared the house with other people but had their own bedroom in the house. I was shocked and relieved when they agreed to rent us their bedroom for one month. It was good to finally have a home base. While it had only been days since Tori and I left the marina, it felt like I'd been uprooted for months, with no sense of home.

It was a large two-storey Victorian home built in the late 1920s, with wide oak plank floors and high ceilings. The bedroom we rented had a picture window that looked out onto the leafy tree-lined street of Brunswick Avenue. There was a queen-sized bed in the room with an enormous photo of the couple – stark naked – on the wall across from their bed. Their frank open eyes, along with all their other organs, seemed to follow you wherever you went. It was a room built for sex. I wasn't comfortable sharing a bed with Neil, but he assured me we were friends, not to worry. His heart (and other body parts) would be waiting until Tori came home. I believed him. I trusted him.

The four other people who lived in the house were much older than me – in their twenties and thirties – and they all played in a rock band too. They practised at all hours of the day and night, making sleep impossible. They were not welcoming. I didn't blame them, since the couple who rented us their room told them that we would be taking over their space for the month just minutes before they left. "Cool" was the response of the guy with the black waist-length hair, as he barely looked up from the kitchen table, where he was rolling a joint.

I didn't venture far from our bedroom, leaving it only when Neil was around. He went off during the day to try to find temporary work. I felt isolated, separated from my friends, especially Tori. I kept in touch by phone with Gary, Leigh, and others who were around in the summer, but it felt like I was in a different world so far from home.

Despite what he'd said at first, Neil began suggesting that since we were sharing a bed, we might as well as enjoy sex together too.

"What about Tori? You love her. It would be wrong to sleep with me. I care about you, but I'm not in love with you like she is," I said.

"We're good friends, and it's only sex. There's sex and there's love. They're different," said Neil.

We had long philosophical talks about the difference between lust and love, about monogamy, and the confines of living within the expectations and rules that society had established as "normal." Aspiring to live the hippie lifestyle, Neil's view on polyamory made sense to me, but I was concerned about how Tori would feel. I would never do anything to hurt her or betray our friendship.

"Let's call Tori," Neil said one night. "We can ask her and see what she thinks about us having sex."

I had spoken to Tori a couple of times since she had been at camp. You had to call and leave a message and then she'd get back to you when she could, usually in the evening.

I was relieved when she called back one day after we had left her a message. I was pretty sure she wouldn't want me to sleep with Neil, and that would be the end of that. We chatted on the phone, catching up on our day-to-day activities. She was busy at camp but looking forward to when she could come home and we could go out west. I told her I was lonely and counting the days. I was so bored. I broached the subject of Neil's idea of free love and what he had proposed.

"Well, what do *you* think of it?" Tori asked.

"I don't know. I like him, but I don't love him, not like you do, that's for sure. Wouldn't you be jealous?"

"No, because you don't have those kinds of feelings for him. I think I'm okay with it," said Tori.

"Really? I don't know, Tori."

"Let me talk to Neil. Put him on the phone."

I sat cross-legged on the floor at Neil's feet while he took my place in the comfy stuffed chair strategically placed beside a little table in the hall that held the phone. I listened while Neil professed his love to Tori; how he yearned for her, missed her. I remained sitting, though every part of my body wanted to flee. I felt like a voyeur eavesdropping on an intimate conversation that was not meant for my ears. I was happy for Tori that she could experience this kind of love, but the twinge in the pit of my stomach revealed an envy that they shared this special bond. I felt like a third wheel in a way that I had never experienced before when the three of us were together.

When Neil explained to Tori that the sex he and I were going to have would not mean anything, my twinge turned to a blow. It was just an understanding between friends, he said. He didn't love me in the same way he loved her. We would move forward only if she was open to it. If not, we wouldn't do it.

After I said goodbye to Tori, I was conflicted. Neil helped me to see this was just a product of how I was socialized about sex and love going together. Tori thought it was fine, and Neil assured me he loved and cared for me, so clearly my apprehension was misguided.

The only time I had had sex was ironically, with Neil's brother, Nedley.

That had not been a pleasurable experience at all. I wondered if sexual prowess was something siblings shared, like eye colour or mannerisms. I was about to find out.

~

INITIALLY, I CHALKED it up to my lack of experience. I must be doing something wrong because Neil seemed to be enjoying sex, but it wasn't so great for me. I considered that I could possibly get pregnant, but wasn't sure what to do about that, how to access birth control, and I was embarrassed to bring it up. Neil never mentioned it. My sister Connie, now a full-time nurse and mother of a young daughter, was the one who talked to me about the pill and helped me get to a clinic. Without her I could have become a teenage mother, like one of the women my mother housed when I was young.

My relationship with Gary was blossoming. He came regularly to visit and I looked forward to being with him. He was kind, open, accepting of me and all I was going through. While he knew Neil and I shared a bed, he did not know we were having sex. I wasn't in love with Neil, so in my mind it didn't feel like cheating — at least that was what Neil told me. When Gary and I talked about taking our relationship to the next level, he mentioned the need for birth control. I had to tell him the truth.

"About birth control," I said one day while we sat outside on the front lawn of the house to escape the incessant throbbing of the rock and roll band inside.

"Yes, if we are going to go further, we need protection," Gary said. "How do you feel about going on the pill? Is it something you could talk to your doctor about? I could go with you."

My heart, which had been pounding with uneasiness about telling Gary I was already on the pill, took refuge in his words. His response was so tender, so caring, so responsible, so unexpected. Would he think I was a slut for sleeping with Neil? Was I? Would he reject me, look at me differently? I was so worried to lose the one foothold I had on a real relationship. I knew I had to risk telling him if I wanted a true connection. He deserved my honesty.

"Actually, I'm already on birth control. I'm taking the pill."

"Really? Well, that's good to know."

"There's more," I faltered, looking without success for words that might soften the blow. "The reason I'm on the pill is because I'm sleeping with Neil."

The small lines between Gary's eyebrows creased, registering this news on his sweet face. He went silent. His head fell downwards, eyes staring at the bent blades of green grass beneath his white running shoes.

I quickly filled in the silence with my rambling defence. "But I don't love Neil at all. I don't even like the sex. I just feel like I have to do it. I don't even want to. I'm not sure why I do it. It's *you* I really care about. Honestly."

"I do love you, Marsha, but I don't know. This isn't right. I'm not going to share you. This guy, Neil, well, he doesn't seem to care about you at all. I don't know why you're with him. I don't get the whole 'going out west' thing. I guess you'll have to make your own decision. I've got to go. Maybe I'll see you later." He got up and simply walked away. He wasn't angry. He just seemed dejected and despondent.

I cried as I watched Gary leave. What was I doing? I felt ashamed, dirty. It was clear I had hurt him. Why hadn't I saved sex for someone special, like Gary, whom I loved? What was love supposed to look like, be like? I was confused. The idea of committing to one person conflicted with what I had grown up with; and with what I was talking about with Neil, and even Tori, who both made the case for a different kind of free love that was more liberating.

That night when Neil made sexual advances toward me, I said no. I didn't want to do that anymore. He persisted. He wouldn't listen to me. I lay on my back, flat as a board on the bed, not moving any part of my body, thinking this would deter him. It didn't. After he finished with me, he told me I needed to engage, move my body around more, if I wanted to be better in bed. He rolled over and then went to sleep, snoring just like his brother.

My rigid body went limp. I wept, feeling like a used-up discarded rag doll. I thought about what Gary had said that day. Why *was* I staying with Neil? He had such charisma and sparkle when Tori and I were together with him on Georgian Bay. The dreams he planted for the three of us to travel and live together were exhilarating, liberating. But now I was living a nightmare, drowning in sorrow and loneliness.

I had to get out.

Chapter 45
Escape

I KNEW THAT WHAT WAS HAPPENING WAS WRONG. I WAS DIStraught at how Neil was treating me with such disrespect. Perhaps I should have said more, explained how I felt, but I was afraid. What if he tried to convince me to stay? He was persuasive and often put things in a way that made me feel like I was too young and didn't understand. Whenever I tried to express my point of view, somehow it never came out clearly, or he twisted my words around and then the meaning wasn't at all what I was trying to convey. It was crazy-making.

I had gotten myself into this mess and I had to get myself out. I couldn't go home again. The thought of Daddy relishing in the knowledge that he was right about Neil would be admitting defeat, like surrendering to my enemy in a war zone. Besides, he had disowned me. Tori was still at camp; how could I tell her that the man she was madly in love with was an asshole. Once again, I turned to Connie, my maternal figure, for assistance. She agreed that I needed to leave and said she'd help me.

I watched through our bedroom window as Neil pulled away from the curb in his beat-up yellow van. The Volkswagen that had once represented sunshine and freedom now evoked symptoms of yellow fever. He said he was going out for a while. I didn't know where he was going, or for how long, but I was ready to make my move. I called Connie on the phone.

"Okay, he's just left. Can you come and get me?" I whispered into the receiver, even though there was no evident need to lower my voice.

"I'm on my way. When will he be back?" Connie questioned.

"I have no idea. Just get here as quick as you can."

There wasn't much to pack, only the clothes I had brought with me. I waited anxiously in the bedroom by the window, watching for Connie's white Datsun. If Neil came home before Connie arrived, I would hide the bag, unpack it later, and try for another day. I had found a rooming house on Delisle Avenue, near Yonge and St. Clair, for ten dollars a week, which was within my budget. I had money saved from my job at Shoppers, as well as the funds Ellen had given me. I could last for several months.

When I saw Connie's car coming down Brunswick, I grabbed my bag and went down the old wooden stairs, avoiding the creaky spots. I didn't want anyone in the house to hear or see me, so when Neil came home they could honestly say they didn't know I had left. I wanted revenge, the satisfaction of inflicting a blow to Neil as he questioned my sudden and mysterious leave-taking.

I loaded my bag into Connie's trunk and sat in the passenger seat. As we pulled away, I could see Neil's familiar van coming down Brunswick. I ducked down in the seat so he wouldn't see me, escaping as if I was a fugitive.

The rooming house on Delisle was a neglected-looking two-storey home in the middle of an affluent neighbourhood. The residents in the house were diverse in age, gender, and race. There were no other white seventeen-year-old girls living there. The landlord showed Connie and me my room on the second floor. Calling it a room would be a misnomer. It had likely been a closet back in the day when one family owned the home. It had a single bed in it and a tiny dresser with two drawers. You had to turn sideways to walk between the end of the bed and the dresser. At least there was a small window. It looked out onto the brick wall of the house next door; no view but at least the window provided light.

The landlord, an older man who spoke little English, told me to always keep my door locked. "The man across the hall from you is just out of prison."

Connie looked at me in terror. Though I felt fear, I had left a situation that was far worse than this one. My sister ultimately had to leave and go home to her family. She said she would be back to visit in a few days. After she left, I sat on the bed, staring out the window at the red-brick wall. While the room was about the size of a jail cell, I felt free from the prison I'd been living in with Neil. I was alone but somehow felt less lonely.

Connie came back as promised a few days later bearing a gift. She opened a large Fabricland plastic bag to reveal dark brown burlap (the material must have been on sale) curtains and a matching bedspread that she had sewn. I sat on the bed, watching her fit the large silver curtain hooks onto the window rod and feeling gratitude for her effort to create a home for me. My snug little room, while not cozy – the burlap proved to be quite scratchy to sit on – was at least colour-coordinated.

Chapter 46
Down and Out

IT WAS WORTH IT TO MAKE THE LONG DAILY COMMUTE TO GET TO my high school at York Mills and Bayview from the rooming house at Yonge and St. Clair. I still had two more years left of school, and my sister's rationale on the value of completing my education resonated with me. Staying in school kept me connected to my friends and I could continue working at my after-school job at Shoppers Drug Mart. Neil had gone out west, not waiting for Tori. She'd decided not to follow him but still wanted to move out of her family home. She chose to live in a different neighbourhood that wasn't close to me — on Walmer Road near Bloor Street. We were still best friends, but she had started to hang out with a different crowd, who I just didn't connect with.

While I maintained my friendships, I felt separate, different from my peers because I was now totally on my own. The privileges that they had, that I had also enjoyed – but had taken for granted – when I was living at home were no longer available to me. Like Tori, I had to pay for rent, food, and transit, leaving little left over for anything else.

If the weather was nice, my friends would come downtown to visit me. They saw my arrangement as desirable, liberating. To them, I had the freedom to do whatever I wanted. This was true, but when they all left to go back to their homes I felt alone, like a child without a family.

Gary and I re-established our relationship. Now that Neil was out of the picture, he recommitted and I came to rely on him: his love, companionship, and availability. I called Gary frequently and came to depend on his daily visits. Initially, he did see me regularly, but it was a long trip by bus and subway and as the demands of homework, after-school sports, and his part-time job began to consume his time, it became difficult. My loneliness fed my neediness. I demanded more of him than he could give. One weeknight when I had been waiting for him to arrive, he called to say it was too late and he wasn't coming.

"Sorry, Marsh, but I just can't make it tonight. It will take me so long to get down there and then get back home. I can't stay over on a school night."

"But I've been waiting for you and *now* you tell me you're not coming. Why didn't you call me earlier?" I asked angrily. "How can you do this to me? It's been so long since you've been here, since we've been alone."

"Well, I can't travel so far all the time. I have stuff to do around home and then there's school."

"But I need you. I'm all on my own here."

"I know."

There was a long silence on the other end of the line. I could hear him breathing, so I knew he was still there. Maybe he felt bad and would change his mind and come.

"Marsha, I think that's part of the problem. You need me too much. I feel guilty if I'm not with you. I can't enjoy just hanging out with my friends. I don't want to feel that. I shouldn't feel that. I can't be with you all the time. I think we should take a little break from seeing each other. It would give both of us some space."

"But I don't need any space," I whined.

"I do," he said.

I loved Gary, was vulnerable with him, trusted him, felt safe with him. I had suffocated the one person I had come to rely on.

The pain of losing Gary was unbearable. I had always felt so self-sufficient and strong, able to weather any storm, but now I was adrift at sea, no compass to guide me. Initially I felt anger that Gary had dumped me; it soon turned to pain and sadness. I understood that the independent girl I had been – the girl he had fallen in love with – had turned into a needy, clingy baby, oozing pity like an open lesion. I didn't like who I had become, so destitute and dependent. If I didn't like myself, how could he?

As hard as it was, I avoided Gary at school and gave him the silent treatment. He tried to be friendly, but I just couldn't reciprocate. It was all or nothing for me.

The maple trees lost their dazzling colours, exposing the stark silhouette of winter, and I had fewer visitors. The novelty of coming downtown had worn off and it was now too cold to sit outside on the front lawn.

I turned to piano for solace. I had missed playing since living on my own. I explored the possibility of seeing whether the church down the street might have a piano that I could use. The minister there was a kind man and he said it would be fine to come and play the piano once a week during the evening, when the church wasn't in use. He said Dennis, the elderly caretaker who cleaned during the evenings, would be grateful for the company and music while he worked. I was glad that I had taken this initiative to continue pursuing piano. It was odd but I thought about how Daddy would be proud of me.

I looked forward to the following Tuesday to start my weekly piano practice. Little did I know that Dennis would be a menace I would have to take on.

~

I WAS SURPRISED one Saturday morning when I saw Renee Seligman, a friend I'd known since junior high, moving boxes into a bedroom on the second floor of my rooming house. She had told me that she was having problems with her parents, particularly her mother, and was thinking about moving out on her own but I had no idea she was considering *my* rooming house. I had mixed feelings about my new neighbour. On the one hand, it would be nice to have a friend for company. On the other, it felt somewhat like an invasion of my space. She never asked me how I felt about it but just assumed it would be okay with me. When our mutual friends who had not visited me in some time came down to see Renee in her room that was much bigger than mine, I was upset and jealous.

One afternoon several weeks after Renee had moved in, I could hear familiar voices coming from her bedroom. There must have been at least six of our friends in there laughing and talking. I waited to see if any of them would come upstairs to see me or invite me down. I was stewing in my room, considering whether I should go and see everyone or boycott her little get-together. I was angry, but mostly hurt about being left out. I decided to be a bigger person, gathering up my pride and courage and walking downstairs to her room.

The door was ajar and inside I could see people spread everywhere: sitting on the bed, the floor, and some standing by the door. Approaching quietly, I first noticed my friends Leigh and Kathy, who were leaning against opposite sides of the doorframe. They greeted me warmly. So far, so good, I thought. I then scanned the room and saw Gary sitting on Renee's bed. My heart sank. A floodgate of feelings unleashed. Anger was first. How dare he come all this way to see Renee, but didn't have time to visit me? Did he even consider my feelings? Then rejection, he doesn't love me anymore.

An awkward silence permeated the room. Everyone knew we had broken up. I could feel heat infusing my body: burning my face, turning to liquid behind my glasses, reaching my armpits, where beads of sweat hung suspended. I had to flee before I became a wet mess. I was able to mumble a lie about needing to be somewhere and fled down the stairs outside, the cold air providing a welcome relief.

Chapter 47
Sunny View

WHEN A LARGER ROOM IN THE HOUSE BECAME AVAILABLE — AT fifteen dollars a week — I seized the opportunity to relocate. Although the physical move was downstairs to the first floor — beside the kitchen — I took it as a sign of upward mobility. The rectangular bedroom surrounded in white-paned glass windows was likely a former sunroom in the original home. While it was minimally larger — I could now fit a chair— it was bright and full of sunlight. I had moved from a closet to a solarium.

Being beside the kitchen had its advantages. I now had easy access to this shared space to cook my meals or make a cup of tea. However, the downside was that the kitchen was noisy, dirty, and smelled like a combination of sour milk and decomposing garbage. The large silver aluminum trash bin — with its lid habitually left off — along with the unwashed dishes in the sink contributed to the smell. The unkempt kitchen was a boon to the cockroaches who feasted on the debris during the night. There was so much I had taken for granted growing up in my sanitary, privileged middle-class home in the valley. I had never seen — never mind lived in — filth like this. Sharing a kitchen with total strangers was daunting. How could I ask people I didn't know — who were much older than me — to clean up their mess or keep the noise down? Sometimes boisterous residents would cook or hang out with friends in the kitchen late at night, making sleep impossible.

One night a female tenant woke me up banging pots around the kitchen while angrily cursing in patois that someone had stolen her food. She hammered on my door and told me to "Open up!" Reluctantly I got out of bed and released my door a crack. She pushed it open, the large whites of her bulging eyes shining back at me. I noticed a thick yellow comb buried deep in her afro, as she began accusing me of throwing out her food. Thoughts of Helen, our unhinged housekeeper who thought my dad was strangling her, flashed through my mind.

"I don't know anything about your food," I said timidly.

"Get out here. Where is my pot that was on the stove that had rice and peas in it?"

"I never saw a pot on the stove. I've been in bed, sleeping," I said, my nightgown and ruffled hair evidence of my slumber.

"I had leftover food on the stove and now it's not there. Where is it?"

"Maybe someone put it in the fridge?" I offered.

"It's not in the fridge, not on the stove, it's nowhere, it's gone. What did you do with it?"

The more I denied that I knew anything about her food, the more intense her rage became. I was terrified. What if she lashed out and hit me? When her boyfriend appeared in the kitchen, my fear deepened. He surveyed the scene and then offered a voice of reason.

"Calm down, Kamile, let's go to bed and we'll deal with this in the morning." Kamile kept on screaming about the missing food and pointing her finger at me, but thankfully her boyfriend was able to guide her back to their room upstairs. She followed dutifully, like a child giving in after a tantrum, continuing to grumble about people in this house taking her things.

Renee heard the noise and came down to the kitchen as they were leaving. Grateful to see someone I knew, I collapsed into her arms, forgetting the petty grudge I was holding against her. Fear trumped pride. I told her about the terror that had just unfolded in the kitchen.

She said not to worry, that she would be an ally if Kamile bothered me again. It felt good to know that I was not alone. It was quite late in the evening, but Renee suggested we go into my room to talk. I agreed, as there was no way I was going to get to sleep with my adrenalin still in fight-or-flight mode.

Renee was beautiful and stylish. Her brown almond-shaped eyes, curvy body, and auburn hair layered in a Farrah Fawcett haircut attracted men wherever she went. She carried herself with a confidence that was enviable, yet underneath the veneer of self-assurance she had insecurities. She had told me some terrible stories of abuse (emotional and physical) inflicted by her mother. One that stood out was when her mom used the cord on the iron to whip her. It was this final humiliation that caused Renee to make the difficult decision to move out.

I missed the intimacy we'd shared before Renee moved in to the rooming house. I was relieved when she raised her concern about our friendship and wanted to discuss what had happened between us. I was able to express the resentment I'd felt since she had moved in. It was scary for me to be vulnerable, to share what now seemed like petty jealousy of the friends who'd visited her, as well as my childish envy of the size of her room. I found it hard to admit I was wrong and to say, "I'm sorry." Apologizing seemed like a weakness to me, conflicting with my desire to be strong, independent, and courageous. Saying sorry felt wimpy. It was, however, a relief to be able to talk to her. Regaining our friendship felt like coming home after a long journey.

Before Renee headed up to her bedroom, she turned to me and said, "You know you should give Gary a call. Talk to him, like you just talked to me. He still loves you, misses you."

"He does? How do you know?"

"He told me. He doesn't understand what he did wrong. Do you still love him?"

"Of course I do." I was heartened by her words. It affirmed that the feelings Gary and I had shared were real, mutual, and perhaps held possibility for the future.

I decided to follow through with her advice and invite Gary to my sunny but somewhat smelly new bedroom.

Chapter 48
Piano Crescendo

WALKING UP THE STEPS THROUGH THE FOUR TOWERING ROMAN pillars to enter the ornate wood-carved interior of the Calvin Presbyterian church almost made me want to convert to Christianity. The beauty and peace in the historic setting provided a welcome calm to my life. I settled into a weekly routine of going to the church every Tuesday evening to practise on the piano. Built in 1927, the church had traditional oak pews, arched stained-glass windows, and high coffered ceilings. As I walked between the rows of empty pews to reach the black baby grand piano that sat in front of the altar, I felt like I was Vladimir Ashkenazy about to perform a solo before an adoring crowd.

When I was ten years old, Daddy took me to see Ashkenazy – an internationally recognized Russian pianist – perform at what was then called the O'Keefe Centre. I don't know how he was able to do this, but Daddy got us backstage after the performance to meet Ashkenazy in person. My father told the famous pianist about my piano studies at The Royal Conservatory. When Ashkenazy turned to me and asked what composers I played, my mind went blank. A small crowd of adults were around us, and they waited patiently for my response. Finally, a name came to mind and I said, "Bach," but I pronounced it with a hard *a* and *ch*, sound, so it sounded like *bayche*. Everyone laughed but I didn't know why. Daddy corrected my phonetic error and laughed along with them. I was humiliated. My one chance at impressing someone famous and I had blown it.

I didn't have a natural ear for piano. I wasn't able to just sit down and play a song, figuring it out from tune and memory. Since I was without music books, my initial sessions in the church focused on practising scales. It felt good to be playing the piano again. I didn't realize how much I'd missed the creative pleasure that playing music can bring.

When I first started practising, Dennis would be there cleaning and he greeted me upon arrival and exit. Then he started to take his breaks when I was there, entertaining me with stories from his past. He had immigrated from Greece, anglicizing his Greek name Daidalos to Dennis. I liked building this connection with an elder because the only grandfather I had known, Sam, had been kind of creepy. I felt safe with Dennis and enjoyed our weekly visits.

Dennis found some sheet music for me to play, so my practice sessions became much more enjoyable and challenging than just working on my scales. He was a captive audience and told me how much he enjoyed my music. Over time he began taking longer breaks and instead of just standing by the piano, broom in hand, he started sitting down on the piano bench beside me. I had trouble telling him that I wanted to spend the time practising, so I came earlier and stayed a little longer to build in time for both piano and conversation.

When Dennis started asking if I had a boyfriend, I was pleased to have an adult interested in my life, but when the questions became somewhat intrusive and he sounded dire warnings – "You have to be careful with boys. They can be bad, dangerous" – I wasn't sure what he meant. When he placed his thick hoary hand on my knee and began stroking my thigh up and down, I learned what he meant by dangerous. The first time it happened I was confused. Was it affection like a grandparent would show to a grandchild? But that vile feeling in the pit of my stomach that I had experienced with Neil surfaced and I knew to listen to it.

I stopped going to the church. More than the loss of piano was the loss of safety, trust, and innocence. This experience contributed to my growing confirmation that seemingly good men could do bad things. There was a pattern developing in my unsavoury experiences, particularly with older men: Neil and now Dennis had violated my trust. My grandfather and father were not such ideal role models either in their treatment of women.

Dennis was a menace, in the true sense of the word. I looked up the meaning of his original Greek name, Daidalos – "cunning worker" – my theory of name and character connection once again affirmed.

Chapter 49
Reunion

THE NOTE ON TORN PAPER WRITTEN IN RED PEN LEFT ON MY BED said:

> "Hi, It's Gary. I came down at 7:30 and you and Renee were out. I came down to see how you were, as I thought I might like to talk to you. I feel that I owe you five million apologies. <u>I still love you</u>. I'm sorry. Let's talk.

I turned the ripped paper over to find the typed rules of the rooming house on the back – which had now left a gaping hole on the bulletin board on the first floor. I reread the note over and over. He still loved me. He wanted to talk. My heart soared. I had not yet had the courage to phone him. The fact that he had come to see me and initiated the visit was more than I could have wished for. I called him right away.

I replaced the scratchy burlap bedspread with a softer floral material in preparation for Gary's visit.

When he entered my sunlit room on a Saturday afternoon, our eyes met, both of us a little unsure how to greet each other after what had been several months of not talking.

"I guess you've seen my new room," I said, extending my arm as if displaying goods on a shelf.

"Yeah, when I came by this week and knocked on your door upstairs, the guy across the hall said you'd moved down here. Don't you lock your door? Seems like a lot of sketchy people live here."

"Not that I have anything to steal, but my lock is broken on the outside. I need to get that fixed."

"I like the new bedspread. Jeez, that brown thing you had was scratchy as hell."

I laughed. Gary always made me laugh. He talked so directly, so honestly. He had no problem saying things you were thinking but would never dare utter out loud. His demeanour helped me to relax. He sat in the rattan chair I had in the corner of the room, while I lay sideways on the bed, my hand propping up my head. We talked for hours, clearing up so many misunderstandings. I listened while he explained what it was like for him to visit me downtown and then travel home by transit in the early hours of the morning. Once, when he arrived home at 4:20 a.m., his parents flipped out and finally put their foot down, saying it had to stop.

I shared how lonely I had felt, cut off from my home, friends, and neighbourhood. Normally so self-sufficient, this neediness was new to me. I didn't like it and I could see why he didn't. I realized that I had put undue pressure on Gary, expecting far too much in wanting him to come and see me every night. I'd been selfish and not seen what it was like for him. He grounded me in the knowledge that what I was going through *was* difficult and that it was okay to ask for help. He wished he could have been more present.

My reunion with Gary was the most joy I had felt since my time in Georgian Bay. The promise Gary and I made to be together, oddly, felt freeing. It was ironic to me that my happiness was derived not from freedom from exclusivity, but the opposite. The sense of commitment felt reassuring. The messages from Daddy, from my world, were: be strong, rely on yourself, don't depend on others. While this had gotten me far, perhaps it had also set up a barrier to connecting with others on a deeper level. A small window of vulnerability opened as I considered Daddy. I hadn't talked to him since that day Neil, Tori, and I had driven away together. Would it always be like this? I didn't want to live with him, but the feeling of being disowned didn't feel good either.

At the time, I could see no way to repair that severed relationship.

Chapter 50
A Real Apartment

RENEE AND I DECIDED TO GET AN APARTMENT TOGETHER AND LIVE somewhere safer, cleaner, and closer to school, friends, and our part-time jobs. We were thrilled when we found an apartment above Smith's drugstore on Yonge Street, north of York Mills – the neighbourhood then known as the "City Limits." It was very close to 77 Plymbridge, so it was familiar territory. Renee worked after school at Canadian Tire and I still had my job at Shoppers Drug Mart. The rent was $150 a month – $75 each – but after reviewing my budget, it was evident that I couldn't afford it. I asked Connie if she could broker a deal with our dad to see if he could contribute. Connie described the squalor I had been living in to Daddy and told him I needed support to continue going to high school. Incredibly, she convinced him to cough up the dough. It was as if a sliver of light had entered through a crack in the closed door of our relationship.

The apartment felt like a real home. Built after the Second World War, it had wooden floors, high ceilings, and was heated with cast-iron hot-water radiators. When it got too hot in the apartment – as it often did – you had to turn a little knob at the back of the radiator and let out some water. We especially liked the privacy because it had its own separate entrance beside the drugstore. At the top of a long flight of stairs, we had two bedrooms – we also used my bedroom as a living room – and a kitchen that could fit a small table. We didn't have much furniture but managed to scramble together two mattresses and some large red foam cushions to make a couch. We found a discarded, but clean, pretty area rug that had a beige background with floral sprays of pink roses, providing the atmosphere of an eighteenth-century sitting room.

We had both become quite skilled at pilfering from our respective employers to provide us with necessary supplies: shampoo, soap, and toilet paper from Shoppers; dishes, coffee maker, and other kitchen tools from Canadian Tire. We shopped legitimately once a week at a collective downtown, our annual monthly membership fee entitling us to fill up jars with peanut butter, rice, and other dried goods.

Since I couldn't afford transit tickets to get to school, hitchhiking was my primary mode of transportation. I wasn't happy with the high school I was going to – York Mills – because I couldn't relate to a lot of the people there. I found it cliquey, exclusive, and basically full of rich Jewish kids. I was a rich Jewish kid too, but given my circumstances I didn't feel like I fit in and I wanted to go to a school that had more diversity. Renee wanted to stay at York Mills, but Tori (who was still living on Walmer Road on her own) and I decided that we would switch schools and go to Georges Vanier, which was in Don Mills, a neighbourhood surrounded by high-rises. It was a longer commute by bus, but we both felt it was worth it to finish grade twelve and thirteen in an environment where we could feel a stronger sense of connection. The school also focused on the arts, so there were opportunities to explore a different type of curriculum.

My childhood friend Glorianne also went to Vanier and had access to her family car. So, Tori, Glorianne, and I set up a routine to meet at the York Mills subway stop and we would carpool to school together every day.

I now lived close to Gary, so we could see each other frequently and easily. We were committed to each other, yet maintained a healthy balance between time alone, time together with our mutual friends, and time alone with our individual friends. It was important to both of us that we remain interdependent, not dependent on each other. None of my friends were in a couple like I was at age eighteen, and I wanted to be sure I didn't miss out on anything just because I was paired with Gary.

Gary had restored my trust in men. He was devoted, tender, caring, and loyal. I felt truly loved and safe with him.

Renee and I settled into a life of domesticity: going to school, working at our part-time jobs, and entertaining our friends on the weekends. Our homegrown marijuana plant provided an affordable way for us to get high. We even got ourselves a black and white kitten. We named her Jasmine, after the Seals and Crofts lyrics in their song "Summer Breeze" – "Blowing through the jasmine of my mind." Life was good.

Chapter 51
Calamity Gary

GARY CALLED TO CANCEL OUR PLANS TO GET TOGETHER THAT DAY and told me he was at the hospital, a Welcome mat attached to his foot.

"What do you mean, a Welcome mat?" I asked.

"I walked into our front door barefoot and somehow the wire from the heavy black rubber mat got lodged into my big toe."

"You're at the hospital?"

"Yeah, my dad took me."

"And the Welcome mat is still attached?" I asked, smiling while I imagined the scene.

"Yeah, it hurts like hell. We couldn't cut the mat off. It is really stuck into my toe, so we just came to the hospital, mat and all."

Gary was accident-prone. Perhaps his brain moved faster than his body because he was often involved in a calamity that caused him some injury. He was always going to the hospital. He didn't need to bring his own welcome mat.

One time, Gary went to Cindy Flandrow's house – who was the most beautiful girl in our high school – to rehearse for a school play they were in together. With her tanned skin, perfect white teeth, blue eyes, and straight shoulder-length blond hair, she looked like a movie star. I was a little jealous when he said he was going to her house, but he assured me I had nothing to worry about; he had no feelings for anyone but me. He said he was apprehensive to go to her fancy house and meet her parents. Gary often felt different or "other" when faced with navigating the class distinctions between himself and his peers. I had never been to his house or met his parents. I think he felt shame about his family's working-class background. I didn't make any judgments about economic status. Sometimes I felt my father had an embarrassment of riches. Why did my family have so much, when others didn't? My time living on my own certainly contributed to my understanding of how challenging it was to make ends meet.

When Gary arrived at Cindy's house to rehearse for the play, her father led him into the living room to wait, directing him to sit in one of a pair of upholstered rocking chairs. Gary, who was nervous, began talking to Cindy's father while rocking in the chair. He must have been rocking a little too vigorously, as he lost control of the chair, causing it to fall backwards off its swivel base, sending him crashing into a sliding-glass door behind him. With shattered glass everywhere, he was lucky he only suffered some small cuts. Whenever I thought about that scene, I would laugh out loud. It was just so typical of Gary. I think Cindy might have been interested in Gary – he *was* good-looking – but his clumsiness might have been more of a deterrent than the fact that he had a girlfriend.

We were in grade twelve when I got another phone call from Gary at the hospital. He didn't sound at all like himself; his voice was flat, mumbled, and far-away-sounding, as if he was calling long distance on a bad phone line. He said he'd been in a car accident. I couldn't understand what he was saying and I hung up the phone, feeling confused and scared.

Gary's best friend Jim shared the details of the collision with me. Miraculously, Jim had no injuries and was released from the hospital, but Gary was in bad shape. They'd been driving on the highway late at night – Jim was driving his parents' Mercury Bobcat – and a truck in the oncoming lane lost control, swerved, and crashed into the passenger side, where Gary was sitting. Gary, who was pinned in the car, had to be removed with the Jaws of Life.

STORM ORPHAN

The next day I went to visit Gary, making the long trek by bus from my apartment to the Richmond Hill Hospital. When I arrived, his parents were by his bedside. It was my first time meeting them and I thought they might judge me harshly considering how often Gary came home from my place in the middle of the night. I was nervous to meet them.

When I saw Gary lying in the hospital bed, worries about my own insecurities vanished. He looked like one of those shrouded mummies I had seen at the Royal Ontario Museum. His right leg in a thick white cast extending from his hip to his toe hung suspended in traction from a massive metal contraption in the ceiling. This was the mother of all injuries. He had broken several bones in his leg. The recovery would be long and arduous. When I heard the grisly details of the collision, I cried with relief that Gary was still alive to tell the tale.

Every day after school I hitchhiked to visit Gary in the hospital.

I got to know his parents, Tom and Norma O'Neill, over the course of his extended hospital stay. They both stood at the side of Gary's bed, letting go of each other's hand whenever I entered the room. Norma's shy smile made me feel that I had a right to be there. Any fear I had that they may have misinterpreted my character soon vanished. I was glad to finally meet them so they could see how much I cared for their son as well confirm that I was not a woman of ill repute.

Gary missed winter that year. He went into the hospital in fall and by the time he came out, it was spring. He had also missed most of grade twelve. He still got all his credits, even though he only went to school for a few months. He also received a cheque from the insurance company for seven thousand dollars, which, at the time, felt like he'd won the lottery. It was often that way with Gary: something bad would happen but he would emerge with an advantage – shit didn't stick to him.

That summer I was yearning to get up north to be by the water. A lot of my friends had their family cottages to go to in the summer, and while I'd been invited for weekends, I craved a longer stay. I asked around but no one wanted – or was able – to rent a cottage with me so I managed to find a small housekeeping cottage near Minden, Ontario, to rent on my own for a week. I lied about my age, saying I was twenty-one, since I didn't think the owners would rent to an eighteen-year-old. Their cottage was on the same property so, while not totally private, it provided me with some comfort knowing that the owners were around should anything go wrong.

My friends drove me to the cottage. They stayed for the day, leaving me there until the end of the week when they planned to come back and pick me up. I packed up our cat, Jasmine, for company and enough food to last the week. I didn't mind being alone in my little cabin. Reading, sitting in the sun, swimming, and enjoying the beauty of the lake was like a tonic to my soul.

Gary, who had come home from the hospital with a smaller cast that went from his knee to his foot, had crutches to get around. He surprised me by hitchhiking all the way up north to be with me during the week. It was true love.

He said it was easy to get a ride.

Chapter 52
A Change of Direction

RENEE COULD SEE NO PURPOSE IN GOING TO HIGH SCHOOL BEYOND grade twelve. She wasn't planning on going to university, and in 1975 Ontario was the only province in Canada that still had grade thirteen, so to her it seemed pointless. She wanted to travel out west with friends, go see my former love Lawrence – whom we both maintained a friendship with – and take a break before figuring out what to do next in her life. This left me alone in our apartment and I couldn't afford it. I asked Tori if she wanted to move in, but due to lack of funds she'd decided to go back home and live with her parents for grade thirteen. Left with no options I, too, had to move home. A part of me felt relief at the idea of going back to live at 77 Plymbridge. Another part of me felt defeat, as if I had failed in my attempt to be totally independent from Daddy.

I had lived on my own for two years and in that time I'd had no contact with Daddy. He never visited where I lived, nor did I go and see him. I did, however, visit his pool from time to time with my friends when I knew he was away travelling. I missed the comfortable life I had taken for granted: food in the fridge, not having to pay bills, a piano to play, a cozy bed, the feeling of walking barefoot on soft carpet when I woke up in the morning. As well as the luxuries, I did miss Daddy. I had overlooked the security that came from having a parent – even an absent one – in my life, someone who had my best interest at heart. It felt wrong to be cut off from him in this way. Going without the material luxuries of home helped me realize the value of money and how hard Daddy had to work, how much he had to earn, to afford a life like ours. He *had* contributed to my rent and Connie did tell me that he always asked about me, was worried about me, so I thought he might be open to a reunification.

Once again, I turned to my older sister Connie to broker the deal and ask Daddy if he would be willing to meet with me to discuss my idea of moving home again. And…could I bring my cat?

Chapter 53
Homecoming

I MOVED BACK HOME WITHOUT JASMINE, MY CAT. TINA, OUR German shorthaired pointer, was getting on in age so introducing a cat was out of the question. I found a friend whose family was more into cats than Daddy. Renee and I also gave away our kitchen stuff, which seemed fitting since it was all stolen anyway. It was hard to say goodbye to Renee, the cat, and my independence.

The first week at home was odd. Daddy and I were awkward with each other, like two people on a first date. We had a conversation about cohabitation rules and what was going to be different.

"I don't want you to have wild parties, like you did before. You can have your friends over, just let me know who is coming and when," said Daddy.

"No, I won't be doing that anymore. I know it wasn't right. I didn't respect you."

"Well, I'm glad to hear you say that. I think it'll work best if we both respect each other. I know you've managed on your own, so I'll try to treat you like an adult, not be so controlling. But there are things I expect, like cleaning up after yourself, helping to look after the house, coming home at a reasonable time."

"I get it, Dad. I'll be responsible."

"Also." Daddy cleared his throat – which meant that something serious was coming – then looked me in the eye and said, "I think we should both try to spend some time with each other. What about having dinner together? Not every night, but regularly."

"Do you mean dinners alone or with Ellen too?" Ellen, now Daddy's steady girlfriend, had not moved in but my absence had allowed her a wide berth. I noticed that her toothbrush and housecoat had taken up residence in his bathroom.

"I mean alone. You and me."

"Yeah, that sounds good."

This was an opportunity for me to make a fresh start. I knew deep down that Daddy hadn't changed, but I had. I no longer felt the all-consuming rage that I had when I lived with him before. My sense of belonging and connection came from my friends, especially Gary, Tori, and Renee. I lowered my expectations of what Daddy was able to give emotionally. He was doing the best that he could and he was trying.

That was enough for me.

~

THE BRASS BED that Lawrence and I lay on for my first romantic encounter was a gift given to me by Daddy for my fourteenth birthday. After Wendy and Connie married, Daddy had surprised me by decorating my new solo bedroom with a collection of antiques. It was an unusual gift for a teenager – my friends weren't impressed – but I was thrilled. The detail, splendour, and provenance of antiques fascinated me.

Across from the hundred-year-old brass bed stood a rich honey-coloured oak dresser from the late 1800s with carved leaf-shaped pull handles on all the drawers. The Victorian engraved wooden love seat he gave me was intriguing because the torn fabric on the cushioned seat revealed evidence of the original straw stuffing inside. At the time, Daddy said he didn't reupholster it so we could choose new fabric together. The vintage furniture also included a dark wooden rocking chair with spool rails that went from the handles to the base. Not a chair of comfort, it was striking because of the intricacy of the carvings, which evoked a time when furniture was handcrafted. Placed at the foot of the brass bed was a large dome-topped trunk panelled with wood and a muted-gold metal floral design. Lifting the lid of the trunk released the smell of musty aged wood, but it was a pleasant odour, like the scent of a secondhand bookstore.

Glued inside the lid was a coloured sketch of a young girl from the eighteenth century. She wore a white smock dress and a red flowered hat that perched on top of her blond ringlets. The picture conveyed a restrained playfulness, with the little girl's feet firmly placed against the bottom rail of a cedar fence, as if she was considering climbing it: one hand on the fence, the other holding her closed floral umbrella, which was the same vibrant red as her hat. I loved imagining that the trunk belonged to this child from another era and wondering what treasures she might have kept inside.

When I moved out on my own, I wanted to claim the furniture – after all, it *had* been a gift – but Daddy said I couldn't take it with me. I was angry at the time, but I could see now that it would have been challenging to move the furniture, never mind trying to fit it all into my small living quarters. Settling back into my bedroom, I found it comforting to be surrounded by this antique furniture again. I noticed that the love seat had been reupholstered in a patterned dark green and gold fabric that suited the era of the piece. I also noticed it had been moved – into Daddy's bedroom. I didn't say anything. There was no point in bringing it up. It wasn't worth fighting about. Besides, it looked nice where it was in his room under the window.

I was proud of my choice to overlook Daddy's small transgression. It was evidence of how I was growing, maturing, and coming to accept Daddy for who he was. There were other annoying things he did: like washing all the pots and pans from dinner *before* we sat down to eat, or repeating stories I had heard a million times. But that was him. He liked a clean house and the familiar stories were ones that gave him joy and comfort.

There was evidence that he was giving both me and the dog a longer leash. Tina no longer had to go out to her pen to sleep every night. On cool nights, Daddy allowed her to sleep in her wicker basket that rested against the dark corkboard wall in the kitchen. She would circle around and around on the cushion inside the basket until finally settling down to sleep, her head tucked into her tail.

Now Daddy made requests, not demands, when he wanted me to do something around the house. He respected my privacy and didn't ask too much about the details of what I was doing. Maybe he was just too scared to ask. I still smoked pot with my friends but I didn't flaunt it. I learned that it was better for our relationship if I was a little more discreet.

Daddy took an interest in what I was doing at school, especially since I was soon going to graduate. We talked about post-secondary options. Those conversations would often get quite contentious because he was adamant about me going on to university. I wanted to take a year off and travel. I applied for journalism at several schools in Ontario. I had an interest in writing, but mostly I did it to keep Daddy quiet. I thought even if I was accepted, I could always turn it down.

When my friends came over, Daddy chatted with them. He was funny, engaging, and charming. He always had been this way, but now I began to notice it. He liked Tori a lot and nicknamed her "Big T." I don't know why he called her this. Maybe because she played such a big role in my life. He got a T-shirt made for her that had "Big T" written on the front. I'm not sure he realized the impact of his choice until after Tori – who was flat-chested – put on the T-shirt displaying the irony.

We followed through on our plan of having regular dinners at home together. Daddy took pride in his cooking, creating unique dishes, no recipes required. I, too, prepared meals but always with a recipe. Like my need for piano sheet music, I couldn't invent but I could follow. While I liked cooking, I got as much pleasure from serving the food. There was a sense of nurturing I felt when I presented Daddy with a dinner I'd made. Occasionally we would go out to eat at our favourite restaurant – The Steak Pit – never wavering from our order of their signature barbecued ribs, with sauce on the side. The familiarity and the predictability were reassuring. Nothing ever changed at that restaurant; not even the waitresses, many of whom had worked there since its opening in 1948.

When Daddy first said, "I love you," I was stunned. He had displayed physical affection toward me and my sisters – hugging and kissing – but I'd never heard him say those three words. It was so direct, so stark. It was strange to see him vulnerable. I couldn't reciprocate. It felt awkward, too soon, too forced. Did I love him? I didn't know. I had been through a lot and while I was coming around, I certainly wasn't ready to gush about love.

I do know that the hatred I felt toward him two years before had evaporated like water on the lid of a boiling pot.

Chapter 54
An Unsettling Goodbye

THE GROSHIPS, WHO HAD LIVED NEXT DOOR FOR NINETEEN YEARS, were moving. Daddy had already said his goodbyes, so when I saw the moving truck loading up on a Saturday afternoon, I went over to wish them well. I walked through the front door that was propped wide open and saw Mrs. Groship leaning on the white kitchen counter, head in her hands. She looked up as I came in. She was crying. It was evident by her puffy eyes and red nose that she had been crying for quite a while.

"Come sit down, Marsha." I sat down hesitantly on one of the two turquoise swivel stools behind the kitchen counter that had yet to be loaded into the truck.

I found it jarring to see adults cry. I had only ever seen Mrs. Groship as a hostess at their parties engaging in small talk. She was effervescent like the drinks Harry, their chef and housekeeper, served to everyone. With her jet-black shoulder-length hair and bright red lipstick, she was always the image of a stylish and modern woman.

I was quiet. I didn't know what to say, so I waited for her to initiate the conversation.

"Oh, Marsha, sorry I'm such a mess. It's so hard for me to leave this house." She unleashed deep sobs and covered her face with both hands, her perfectly manicured fingernails providing a stark contrast to her disarray.

"Well, why are you moving? I mean, do you have to move?"

She wiped her face with a white cloth handkerchief, the small letters SG engraved in black cursive lettering on the corner. I only ever called her Mrs. Groship, but I knew her first name was Sylvia. I thought everything about her was elegant, tasteful, and classy.

"Oh dear. Mr. Groship isn't well. The house is so much work. I know it's time to move on but, well, life is complicated. We built this house just like your father built yours. It will always be home. You're young and have your life ahead of you, Marsha. Enjoy every precious moment."

Mrs. Groship was rambling, but it felt like she was trying to convey something important to me. She then started saying things about her husband and the life choices she had made. I didn't understand the meaning of what she was trying to communicate and it made me feel uncomfortable. She was crossing a boundary and sharing things that seemed too intimate. I felt sorry for Mrs. Groship, but it also felt creepy and I wanted to leave. I stood up to go and she came from behind the counter and gave me a big hug, holding me tightly in her arms for a little too long.

"Thank you for coming to say goodbye, dear. It means so much to me."

I walked back to our house next door feeling uneasy about what I had witnessed and experienced. There was also a sense of familiarity. When else had I felt like this? My mind flashbacked to when I was nine years old. It was the goodbye Carol gave me the night before she died.

I hoped Mrs. Groship would be okay.

Chapter 55
New Neighbours

GETTING CONTACT LENSES WAS LIBERATING. THE OPHTHALMOLOgist said I would be a good candidate for contacts as my vision was so poor (without glasses I was considered legally blind), but I would have to wait until my eyes stopped growing. At nineteen I was finally ready.

The first time I put them in it felt like I had golf balls in my eyes. It would take a while to adjust. To build up my tolerance, I gradually increased the amount of time I wore them over several weeks. I followed a very precise routine. I used the same small blue hand towel, laid it out flat on the bathroom counter, assembled the cleaning and wetting solution on the towel, and then leaned over the magnifying mirror, careful to look only at my eyes, not the countless pimples on my chin, or that would lead me down a path of distraction. It took me fifteen or twenty minutes for the whole procedure. If I spent too much time trying to get them in, I would tense up, my eyes would dry out, and then I wouldn't be able to insert them at all.

I felt free and unencumbered without glasses, like the sensation of nakedness when you first remove all your clothes at night before bed. I also liked how I looked without frames blocking my eyes. I had curly hair that rested on my shoulders but was short at the front. My hair seemed to fluctuate from straight to curly every several years (hormonal, I guess), but I was loving the curly look. I wanted to look like Carole King.

A girl my age moved in next door and I thought *she* really did look like Carole King, long curly hair and all. Her name was Mary Moore and she was cool. She was the opposite of that other Mary Tyler Moore on TV. She was tall and large yet carried herself with grace. Mary made inhaling a cigarette look like a thing of beauty. She didn't hide the fact that she smoked from her parents, lighting up whenever she wanted and leaving telltale butts with red lipstick stains in ashtrays around her house. She was quiet but not in a shy way. You could tell she was watching, observing, and learning things about people, which gave her a certain kind of power. I saw her walking to school every day and I wanted to join her, but I was intimidated and didn't quite know how to approach her. Leigh ended up becoming good friends with Mary so she introduced us. Mary's family were as different as could be from the Groships. The Moores transformed the Groships designer-decorated home with modern furniture into a comfortable, relaxed atmosphere with big flowered chintz cushions on the sofa and colourful painted cupboards in the kitchen. The parties they had were loud, wild, and saturated with alcohol.

Mary had a lot of responsibilities. She had to cook dinner for her parents, her older sister Laura, and younger brother Paul every night. No hired chef for them. Mary was free labour. Her mother said she'd prepared meals her entire life and simply wasn't going to do it anymore. She worked full-time as a nurse and that was enough to manage. Mary's Dad was big like her and always seemed happy. I'm not sure what his job was, but he took socializing very seriously. I got to know Mary and went to quite a few parties at 79 Plymbridge. There would be all ages at the Moores' parties: the parents' friends, the kids' friends, and the neighbours. Daddy never went to any of their parties. He wasn't into being around people who were drinking.

While I stayed out late consuming alcohol and sleeping in until noon on weekends, Daddy kept himself on a regular routine of downing his nightly choice of drinks – Metamucil. He was in bed by 10:00 each night, so he could wake up on time for his daily 6:30 morning jog, with Tina at his side.

Chapter 56
Fireworks

ON VICTORIA DAY WEEKEND, THE VALLEY NEIGHBOURHOOD Association always put on fireworks for all the residents. They were held in a small park that was right beside Leigh's house, so we would go early to Leigh's for snacks and then get a good viewing spot. When word got out about the free fireworks and people from other neighbourhoods started to attend, the association had to move them to a larger park in Hoggs Hollow. It was a special night, and hundreds would come to share in the spectacle.

In 1976 the fireworks were meaningful since not only did they mark the beginning of summer, but also the end of high school for me. I had only one more month left of seeing my friends every single day and then who knew where we would all disperse?

I had worked my way up to wearing my contact lenses all day and was wearing them for the first time at night at the fireworks. Gary, Tori, and my entire group of friends from school and the neighbourhood came. It was a magical evening of togetherness. I've always loved fireworks: the loud bang as they initially release and then the quiet puff sound in the air when the glittery stars reveal themselves – the shimmery gold ones are my favourite. I especially enjoy the sound of the crowd oohing and aahing together after each pyrotechnic display. The sense of community when a crowd experiences something together evokes a tenderness in me. It is why I go to a theatre to see a movie.

I feel connection, hope, and unity when a shared human experience breaks down barriers of difference.

Since Daddy was away travelling for business in South Africa and wasn't due home until later that night, I lingered at the fireworks.

The next school day it was hard to wake up early for my morning contact lens ritual. I was excited to show Daddy how I was now wearing them all day because when he'd left over a week ago, I was still wearing them intermittently.

I went downstairs for breakfast to find Daddy lying on his stomach on the kitchen floor: arms under his head, feet crossed. He was at the end of the kitchen and it looked like he had chosen this spot to have a little rest.

"Hi, Daddy. What are you doing?" I asked, thinking he was going to pop up any second and scare me as a joke.

No response.

He was wearing his blue Adidas jogging suit and it was 7:30, so he'd already been for a run. I thought he must be tired after getting in from his trip in the middle of the night. Still, it was weird that he would sleep on the floor like that.

"Dad? Daddy? Do you hear me? Wake up. It's not funny." I inched closer for a look and stiffened. His face was ashen, lips blue. I couldn't tell if he was breathing or not. I couldn't move. My feet – my entire body – went rigid, as if encased in cement or stuck in mud.

"Daddy? Daddy?" I screamed. I knew I should go to him, shake him, see if he was breathing or not, but I just couldn't. I couldn't touch him, I couldn't even look at him. Fear, panic, and shock hijacked my brain. I tasted sourness in my mouth as if my spleen had erupted.

There was a phone in the kitchen. I looked at it, but my feet wouldn't move. I needed help. Who could help? Connie. I needed to call Connie.

I don't know why I didn't think of calling an ambulance. Connie was a nurse and she would know what to do. I also couldn't use the phone in the kitchen. It didn't make sense, but I thought what if Daddy hears me talking and I scare him.

I ran to the den, called the number I knew so well, and could barely talk. Knowing that something was off as it was early in the morning on a weekday, Connie immediately said, "What's wrong?"

"It's Daddy. He's on the floor in the kitchen. He won't get up. I don't know what to do."

"Is he breathing?"

"I don't know. I'm too scared to touch him. His lips are blue."

"Okay, I'm on my way. I'll call an ambulance. Go next door and get Mrs. Moore to come over."

I hung up the phone and ran out the front door, avoiding looking in the kitchen. I could tell from my peripheral vision that Daddy was still lying there, motionless.

I banged on the Moores' front door. No answer. I kept banging continuously until Paul, Mary's brother, slowly opened the door.

"Oh, hi, Marsha. How's it going?" he said casually, as if I was making a social call at 7:30 in the morning.

"Where is your mom?"

"I don't know. I just got up."

"It's an emergency. Something is wrong with my dad."

"Oh, okay, I'll go get her."

I waited on the porch with their front door open, for what seemed an interminable length of time.

"She's in the shower," Paul said as he ran back to the front door.

"Get her out. I need her now. My dad, he's… he needs help."

"Don't worry, Marsha, I'll get her to come over right away."

Now what? I didn't want to go back inside my house. Too scared. I couldn't look at Daddy. I waited in limbo, somewhere between the Moores and home.

Connie arrived before Mrs. Moore. I followed her as she rushed into the house, threw her car keys on the floor, and without any hesitation rushed to Daddy, rolled him onto his back, and began doing mouth-to-mouth resuscitation. Mrs. Moore then came running in and began helping Connie.

I waited on the sidelines immobile, standing in the kitchen doorway far away but close enough to see the yellow bile coming out of Daddy's mouth. Connie cleared it away with her fingers and then continued pressing her mouth against his, blowing her breath into him at regular intervals. She was no longer Daddy's first-born daughter but a nurse doing her job.

Mrs. Moore looked up at me, standing there, and said, "Marsha, where is the phone book, the white pages?

"In the den."

"Do you know the name of your father's doctor?"

"Yes, Dr. Feldman."

"Okay, I need you to go to the white pages and look up Dr. Feldman's number. Can you do that?"

"Yes," I said, glad to have a task that would take me out of the kitchen and give me a purpose.

There was only one phone book for all of Toronto back then, so it was a massive heavy tome that had to be placed on a tabletop to navigate. I found the book in the place Daddy always kept it – the bottom drawer of the built-in desk – and pulled it out. What had Mrs. Moore asked me to do? I couldn't think straight. Was Daddy still alive? Why did all that stuff come out of his mouth? Was that a good sign or not? My hands were shaking, making it difficult to turn the thin white pages of the phone book. I had to find a doctor... Daddy's doctor. I began the arduous task of going through the alphabet in my mind. Doctor Feldman. First find the letter *F*. What was next? I couldn't concentrate. I was afraid I wasn't working fast enough. They need the doctor's number. Why did Mrs. Moore give me that job? What if I can't find it? Focus. There are so many Feldmans. Which one? I carried the heavy book into the kitchen. "I don't know which Dr. Feldman it is," I yelled to Mrs. Moore.

"Just keep looking," she said. This didn't make sense. How can I find it? They were still hovering over Daddy.

"Marsha, just go in the den and do your best to find that number," said Mrs. Moore.

It seemed like it was important, so I just followed her orders and went back to the den, gazing in a stupor at all the doctors named Feldman.

I didn't see or hear the ambulance arrive. I only remember getting in Connie's car and following it. Why was the ambulance siren not on? That couldn't be a good sign.

"Is Daddy going to die?" I asked Connie.

"I don't know. We'll find out more when we get to the hospital."

This made sense to me and gave me hope that maybe he was going to be okay.

I didn't think about Connie's feelings at the time. What must it have been like for her to come into that scene and try to revive what I now know was our dead father? She was composed and it made me feel like everything was going to be alright.

When the ambulance pulled ahead – leaving us stuck behind a garbage truck– was when I noticed Connie starting to unravel. She leaned on her horn, yelling at the truck driver to move, but this seemed to have the opposite effect. The workers waved and walked as if in slow motion, lifting the garbage cans first from one house then the next as if they had all the time in the world. Connie rolled down her window and started yelling, "Jesus, can't you move your truck? We need to get by."

I looked out the window and watched while the weekly pickup of trash continued, the mundane minutiae of life carrying on as if this job was important while I sat in a car waiting to find out if my life as I knew it was over.

∼

WHEN WE FINALLY got to North York Hospital, there was a maze of parking, hallways, and nursing stations we had to navigate – that Connie navigated. We ended up in a small room, where a nurse told us to wait. "The doctor will be with you shortly."

Connie, a nurse who knew the hospital system well, wasn't going to wait. "An ambulance just brought our father in, Gilbert Barrett, heart attack– is he alive?"

The nurse repeated her mantra. "The doctor will be in shortly and will go over everything with you."

Connie was no longer calm. "Just tell us, if he's dead or alive. I know you have that information. I'm a nurse. We're not waiting in here for a doctor to tell us that," she screamed.

The nurse went quiet, looked at us both while we waited expectantly. "I shouldn't really do this, but I'm sorry to say your father has died. The doctor will be with you momentarily."

The nurse turned and walked away, leaving us both in the sterile white room standing up and sobbing, holding on to each other, as the familiar pain of death, loss, and grief crept back into our bodies.

Daddy was fifty-four years old, about to celebrate his birthday in less than a week.

I was nineteen and would now be on my own – an orphan.

Chapter 57
Life and Death

I OFTEN THINK ABOUT HOW I WAS UPSTAIRS IN THE BATHROOM putting in my contact lenses, taking all the time in the world, while my father lay downstairs dead on the kitchen floor. I don't feel guilt or ask myself what if. What if I hadn't taken so much time? Could I have gotten to him sooner and saved him? I could not have acted any differently than I did – with shock, fear, and panic. It's more the concept of time itself and what I gave value to that causes me to reflect. I was being meticulous about something I thought was so important, while a life – my father's life – was ending. These two things happened in the same house at the same time.

I imagine the scene as if in a movie, the young teenage daughter upstairs preening in front of a mirror, so critical that she look just right for school, while unknown to her, her father downstairs suffers pain silently, as he lays himself down to die. Did he call out? Did he know he was having a heart attack? Why did it look as if he had just laid down to have a sleep? What was he thinking, feeling? How long was he lying there? These are questions that consumed my thoughts for many years.

Now, as an adult, I have come to terms with my father's death and these unanswered questions. I value time and the preciousness of life in a way I never did before. When I found Daddy on the kitchen floor that day – my world, my life, changed forever.

The juxtaposition of celebrating the fireworks days before burying Daddy seemed odd. How could life be so joyful one moment and so excruciating the next? Such a thin line between ecstasy and agony.

The funeral was at Temple Emanuel, with Rabbi Bielfeld delivering the eulogy. Connie, Saul, Wendy, and I waited in the black limousine outside the temple entrance. Wendy and Steve had divorced several years earlier when Wendy came to the realization that she was in love with the maid of honour, not the groom. Steve came to the funeral but his place in our family no longer existed.

I watched – invisible behind the tinted glass of the car window – while the people in Daddy's life and mine walked up the concrete stairs to enter the temple. I was touched that so many of my friends had taken the day off school to come and pay their respects. When I saw Gary, I just wanted to go and be with him, sit with him. He had come over to my house as soon as I called to tell him the news. I was grateful to be able to count on him.

Then I saw a flash of Brenda. Other than her long hair, she looked the same. She was wearing that telltale quizzical look on her face and inappropriate clothing – a black dress but one that exposed her cleavage. As she quickly entered the temple, I wondered how she felt. I wanted to look at her longer. I would have liked to talk to her to find out what her life was like now, but much more than the limousine separated us.

The family of the deceased must wait to enter the temple until the entire congregation is seated. This Jewish ritual seems insensitive. Like a wedding, we're expected to walk down the aisle on display to take our seats at the front, except we're wearing black and not looking so great. When it was time to go down the aisle, I felt sick to my stomach, the saliva pooling in my mouth. I said to Wendy, "I can't do it. I'm not going."

"You have to go."

"I'm going to barf."

An acid taste of puke entered the back of my throat. My legs were shaking and I felt weak. I had taken Valium the night before so I could sleep and I still felt groggy. The walk from the entrance to our seats looked insurmountable.

"Connie and Saul will go first. Grab my arm. Don't look at anybody, just look straight ahead."

"What if I throw up?"

"You won't. Trust me. I'll hold you all the way."

I grabbed on to Wendy for dear life, praying to a God I didn't believe in that I wouldn't flip my breakfast cereal, or pass out.

I made it without incident to the chair in the front row and gratefully sat down in front of the bimah where Rabbi Bielfeld stood, looking down at us.

The rabbi knew my father well and had been through quite a lot with him: Carol's Jewish conversion and suicide, Brenda's attempt at both conversion and suicide. While they had been through some painful moments together, these experiences didn't create a bond. The two men didn't like or respect each other. Daddy would often talk disparagingly about Rabbi Bielfeld to anyone who would listen. Our family no longer belonged to the temple, since Daddy had left after a fight with Rabbi Bielfeld, so Connie had to plead with him to conduct the service. She convinced him that the service was for us and he relented.

Rabbi Bielfeld, who now had the floor and no fear of retribution from my father, delivered a eulogy that certainly didn't glorify Daddy. On the contrary, he spoke of a man who had an "inability to love others." He went on and on, first creating discomfort and then ultimately anger. It was okay for us as family to highlight Daddy's shortcomings, but for a rabbi, at his funeral?

After the service, Saul, Connie, Wendy, and I went home to 77 Plymbridge to debrief in the den. I gazed at Daddy's guns and pipes surrounding us in the pine-panelled room, trying to come to grips with the finality of his death. How could he be gone? I felt numb and kept thinking this was all a big mistake. It seemed like he was on a business trip and would be back soon. We all took turns telling stories about Daddy, moving between bouts of tears and fits of laughter, the two spirits of sorrow and comedy mixing together like a Shakespearean cocktail. I wondered if it was okay to laugh at the same time you also felt grief? We shared our mutual shock at the rabbi's insolent eulogy. How could he speak so poorly of Daddy? He didn't deserve that, nor did we. A funeral is as much for the living as it is for the deceased, and we were all left with a feeling of anger, not peace. But most shocking of all was the news that Saul shared.

"Before the service, the rabbi told me that a man named Derek had approached him, introducing himself as your father's 'illegitimate' son."

Chapter 58
A Brother

AT THE TIME OF DADDY'S DEATH, I DIDN'T KNOW THAT HE'D HAD extramarital affairs – with the mother's helpers or anyone else. I believed that my parents' marriage was sacrosanct. Daddy described it that way. He always said that he and my mother had a perfect marriage. The copies of my mother's letters that I read as a young adult – the ones she had sent to her brother Stan– certainly confirmed this. She talked about my father in a loving way and her life seemed charmed. There was no evidence of any permeable cracks in the description of her life. So, when Saul revealed the news of my father's *illegitimate* son – which was the term used at the time – I was stunned. Connie, nine years older than me, remembered our parents fighting about a woman and my mother telling him to stop seeing her, so she was not surprised. Wendy, like her birth order, was in the middle. She didn't remember any fighting, didn't know about this specific affair, but wasn't surprised by the news of our philandering father cheating on our mother.

The rabbi wasn't sure what to do when Derek approached him at the funeral, so he directed him to Saul. Before the service even started, Derek had informed Saul that Gilbert Barrett was his father and he wanted to meet his half "sisters." Saul was flabbergasted and waited to tell us this news until after the funeral.

We all questioned the legitimacy of this man. "How old is he? How do we know he isn't just making it all up?" I asked.

"Well, first off, he looks exactly like your dad," said Saul. "He has the same dark skin and facial features: nose, eyes, everything. There is no doubt he is your father's son. He's the same age as Wendy, twenty-five – born the exact same year and month."

I tried to take in this news. I was in a state of suspended disbelief. So many conflicting emotions all at once: confusion, anger, betrayal, grief. I didn't know how to process it all.

Wendy, ever the curious one, posed more questions. "What did he say? What does he want?"

"Well, my guess is he wants money," said Saul, a lawyer and now also the newly appointed executor of my father's estate. "Derek said he tried meeting with your father over the years, but your father refused – he disowned Derek and would have nothing to do with him."

"I don't want to see him," said Connie. "He never knew Daddy, had no relationship with him, why meet him now?"

"I don't want to either," I said.

Wendy was the holdout. "Well, I think we should meet him. At least once. Find out what his story is. Aren't you curious to see what he looks like?"

We decided that Saul would contact Derek to set up one meeting – Connie was firm on that – to satisfy our curiosity – mostly Wendy's curiosity – but that was it. Nobody wanted to establish a relationship with this guy. I had no empathy for him. I thought he was thoughtless and selfish for choosing this time, our time of mourning, to crawl out of the woodwork. I never considered what his life had been like shut off from any relationship with his father.

Derek came to Connie and Saul's house several weeks after Daddy's death. It was eerie seeing a younger version of our father walk into the room. Saul's description was accurate. Derek not only looked like Daddy but also a lot like Wendy. We were all speechless and grateful to let Saul take the lead in directing the conversation.

Derek came with a scrapbook full of newspaper clippings that he had collected over the years to piece together a story of who his father was. The amount of press Daddy had – around golf, business news – was as surprising to me as Derek's collection of it. His mother had been a cocktail waitress at the Brunswick House when she met my father. She had encouraged Derek to come forward when she read the news of Daddy's death in the newspaper.

I tried to imagine what it would have been like for my mother knowing that her husband was having a baby with another woman at the same time as *she* was about to have their second child. I don't know if she knew this at the time or not. My guess is that Daddy never told her, which is why he didn't want any relationship at all with Derek. Derek said "our" father had cut off all ties with his mother when he found out she was pregnant. All he knew about him was from what his mother had told him and the press clippings. As a young adult, he had tried to connect with my father, showing up unannounced at his office. Daddy turned him away and told him never to contact him again.

Our visit ended with Derek saying he would like to meet again. Neither Connie nor I were interested, but Wendy shared her phone number, encouraging him to call. Wendy empathized with the injustice that Derek had experienced. He had been raised by a single mother with limited means and Wendy, aware of our privileged life, felt he deserved more. They got together a few times, but when his phone calls and desire to establish a familial connection intensified, Wendy let him know that she wasn't interested in pursuing a relationship.

Derek's appearance unearthed a secret that Daddy thought he would take to his grave. It was a different time then. An affair was a scandalous thing. What if he hadn't kept it hidden? What might have been different for our family, for Derek and his mother, for Daddy?

After all, he had always wanted a son.

Chapter 59
Robbed

THE MEASUREMENT OF TIME IS A CURIOUS THING. IN THE OLYMPICS, less than one-tenth of a second can secure a gold medal. No one remembers the athlete who didn't win, yet they were often only milliseconds away from glory. There is a minuscule moment of time like this when you wake from nighttime sleep to morning consciousness. It's when your brain doesn't yet register your current reality. If you're not aware of it, you will miss it. If you have ever suffered loss or trauma, you will know this moment. It is fleeting but welcome. Then, in less time than it takes to blink your eye, it is gone and the consciousness of the excruciating pain of your life floods back into awareness.

Daddy's sudden death created emotional and physical turmoil for me, but outwardly I showed only calm containment. I was afraid of unravelling like a loose thread pulled from a sweater. Be strong and self-reliant. This was the message I had grown up with. The image of Daddy lying on the floor and Connie's attempt at resuscitation played over and over in my head. It caused nightmares and an irrational fear of sleeping on my stomach. I trained myself to sleep on my side because I thought I might die if I slept in the same position as I found Daddy. I never talked to anyone about it, never cried, never went through a mourning process. After the funeral, people came to the house to sit shiva and I went through the motions of grief but didn't let myself feel anything.

One evening my Aunt Cynthia, my father's sister, joined me at the kitchen table, where I was sitting with friends who had come to the shiva. She kept talking *at* me, trying to penetrate my wall of defence. I wasn't close with my aunt and her so-called "concern" didn't seem genuine. She badgered me with questions: "Who was I talking to? Did I have support? What was I going to do? Where would I live? This was going to be so difficult for me. Have you cried yet?"

I avoided responding and instead focused my gaze on Tina in her basket, as she circled around and around unsuccessfully trying to find her cozy resting place. I could identify more with the dog than with my Aunt Cynthia. I couldn't settle either. Poor Tina, how would she cope without her master?

Then, my aunt yelled out, "You're an orphan now!" desperately trying to get a reaction from me.

It worked. Tears streamed down my face and the lump in the back of my throat, which I had closed like a locked safe, clicked open. Aunt Cynthia got up from the kitchen table to come and hug me. I was repulsed. I remained sitting and turned my body to stone.

"Yes, it's good to cry, Marsha. Let it out, it's important to grieve."

She then left me in that unravelled state, satisfied that she had done her work and broken me down. I was angry and confused. How was letting my guard down helpful? I needed my armour if I was going to get through this battle.

It was as if I had woken up in a foreign country that I hadn't planned on visiting, hadn't packed for. I didn't know how to navigate or ask for directions or help. I didn't even know what help I needed. My most pressing concern was finishing high school. I still had one month left. Where would I live? Connie and Saul lived in a small semi-detached house with two young children aged two and half and one and a half. They decided to move into the house with me, but Connie said staying there was "creepy," so they left. Also, it just wasn't practical for them because Connie was busy with her own family as well as full-time work. Wendy lived downtown in a house she rented with a group of friends, which was too far for me to commute to school. Tori stayed with me but after a while her parents said it was time to come home. Gary's parents asked if I wanted to come and live with them, but I didn't know them that well – I had only spent time with them when Gary was in the hospital. I decided to live in the house on my own until I finished school. I was scared, but it was the only place that felt like home. Besides, someone needed to be there to look after Tina, our dog. She kept me company for a while. It was unsettling how the dog reacted to Daddy's absence: whining in a high-pitched tone for no reason, going to the back door and then turning back, looking for Daddy to let her outside. I'd let her out and she would immediately bark and scratch at the door wanting to come back in. She spun around in her basket, first in one direction and then another, like a washing machine stuck on the agitation cycle. It was uncanny when, only weeks after Daddy's death, Tina suffered the same fate as him and dropped dead of a heart attack.

I never felt more alone in my life.

Gary hung out with me after school, but I was on my own a lot. It was bleak and especially frightening at night.

One Saturday morning I woke up and noticed the door to Daddy's bedroom was open. I kept it closed, a literal way of shutting out anything that might trigger grief. I walked in to find the glass in the window shattered and his television gone. The clock that shared the same electrical outlet as the TV was flashing 2:30 a.m. – I guess the backup battery had worked for a while. Someone had broken into the house in the middle of the night and stolen Daddy's TV.

I called Gary, and then I called the police to report the robbery. Gary was with me when the two uniformed cops showed up and went through the house. I wanted them to find the person who had done this so I could feel safe, but at the same time I was terrified that they might discover someone hiding in the house. The officers took me seriously and went into every room as if they were looking for the thief. When they got to the living room, the closed curtains had a rounded shape at the end. It looked as if someone was hiding behind the curtains. One cop drew his gun while the other swiftly pulled back the curtains in one deft movement.

No one there. I breathed. The heating vent had caused the curtains to billow. The police did a thorough search, reporting that no one was in the house and said that whoever did break in was likely someone who knew what they wanted, as only the TV was missing. This was worse than a random stranger. It was alarming to know it was premeditated by someone who had been in our home, someone who knew Daddy had died and had a TV in his bedroom.

Gary said he would get me a gun.

Chapter 60
Florida Escape

GARY'S FRIEND RON HAD ACCESS TO A GUN AND SAID I SHOULD have this so I could protect myself. While I was afraid for my safety, I couldn't imagine holding a gun, never mind firing one. Gary tried to convince me that just having it there, not using it, might deter someone.

"What if they took the gun and then turned it on me? I don't even know how to use a gun."

"Ron can show you. He said he would come over."

It had come to this. I felt like I was living in an apocalypse. Not only was my world destroyed, but now I had to defend my place in it.

"No way. I don't want a gun."

"I am worried about you, Marsh. Being here all alone. What about the window? It's broken, anyone can get in now."

We boarded up the window. Now the outside of the house was beginning to reflect my own deterioration. I don't know how I got up and went to school every day, but I managed to graduate from high school.

Mrs. Stinson, my childhood pseudo-mother, had become a real estate agent, so when Connie chose her to sell the house it was comforting to know that she would be handling all the details. It was painful to watch prospective buyers come through. I could no longer tolerate living there. When high school finished and my friend Kathy Sniderman suggested we take a trip to Florida, I jumped at the chance to get away. Kathy's mother and stepfather, Sydney, owned a condo in Longboat Key, Sarasota. They said we could go for an extended length of time. Gary, Kathy's boyfriend Paul, and another friend, Debbie, came as well. The condo was lavish, not only because of its beautiful interior with white leather couches, Sydney's modern art on the walls, and the crashing waves on the beachfront lulling us to sleep, but also because it allowed me the luxury of not having to think about Daddy: his death, home, or what I was going to do with my life. The heat in Florida in the middle of July warmed every part of my being and kept me in the moment. We also had fun. I couldn't remember laughing or drinking so much. My discovery of a new cocktail called Good and Plenty (made of ouzo and kahlúa) was an apt description of the special time Gary and I shared together.

We rented a car and drove down to Miami and Key West, staying in cheap motels along the way. There were no difficult decisions to make, no challenges to deal with, other than a trip to the hospital in Longboat Key as Calamity Gary had to make his presence known there. He fell while waterskiing and the tibia in his leg – where he had pins inserted after the car accident – started causing pain. There was no new injury, so after getting some painkillers, he was fine.

When it was time to go home, I didn't want to leave. There was still a month of summer left and I had decided that I wasn't going to go to Carleton University in Ottawa for journalism in the fall. I didn't want to go to school at all. I didn't know what I wanted. I just knew I wanted to keep travelling. Gary and I decided to continue our vacation and go to California together. We both had saved money from our part-time jobs, Gary's insurance money from the car accident had materialized and we could travel on the cheap – hitchhiking and sleeping in a tent. We booked a flight to Los Angeles – too far for us to hitchhike there. We weren't going to rough it that much. I was thrilled. California, here we come!

Chapter 61
California

WE LANDED IN L.A. AND SPENT OUR FIRST NIGHT IN A MOTEL SO WE could do some of the touristy things: a tour of the stars' homes in Beverly Hills and a visit to Universal Studios. It took a big bite out of our budget, but it was worth it to see the real "Jaws" leap out at us as a boat navigated us behind the scenes of the making of the 1975 hit movie. *Jaws* was one of the films that had been showing when I worked at the movie theatre. All the staff would have such fun counting down the seconds to the two precise moments in the film when the audience would scream predictably as Jaws leapt out of the water.

We purchased supplies in L.A.: a small pup-tent, some canned food, a big bag of peanuts in the shell for protein, and then headed out to hitchhike up the US 1 Pacific Coast Highway. Our plan was to stay at campsites along the way, eventually ending up in San Francisco. It was August and we had one month to do whatever we wanted before any life decisions had to be made.

Back then it was safe to hitchhike, and we met friendly people who told us of inexpensive campsites where we could stay for fifty cents a night or offered us places to stay in their own homes. One guy who gave us a ride said he had to go to work, but he shared his address, told us where the key to his house was, and said he would keep his German shepherd in the bathroom, so we could go in whenever we wanted. Another time when we were on a stretch of highway near Morro Bay that was not well travelled, we stood at the side of the road for a full day without getting a ride. It was starting to get dark when the owner of the Leeward Motel, who had seen us standing there, came out to help us. His motel was full but he said we could sleep in his boat, which was outside the motel. He invited us in for a drink and then ended up giving us a room since someone had cancelled. We did pay for it but it was worth it to be able to sleep on a bed and have a shower.

We weren't prepared at all for camping. We had bought canned goods to cook over a fire but overlooked the fact that we would also need a can opener. One night we walked into a town near Pismo Beach, where we were camping, to purchase a can opener and decided to go out for dinner. It was a real treat to eat in a restaurant, especially since we had been consuming a lot of peanuts in the shell. Our idea of purchasing inexpensive protein packed nuts had proven to be a bad choice. It took a long time to break all those shells to get two tiny peanuts and then there were the shells to deal with. We were grateful to have a hot meal with the bonus of a doggie bag of leftovers to take back to our tent. We didn't consider that you shouldn't keep food in a tent. I woke up in the morning and even though I had minimal vision without my glasses, I could see a blurry line of movement along the seams of the tent.

"What's that?" I asked Gary.

"What?" Gary said, groggy from sleep.

"There on top of the tent. It looks like something is moving."

"Holy shit! Ants. They're everywhere"

We sat up and followed the trail of ants to the white bag we had brought home from the restaurant. No longer white inside, it was a black moving infestation of ants. We had to buy cans of Raid to spray the tent, sleeping bag, and all our clothes.

The highlight of the trip was our time in Big Sur. We were fortunate to get a ride in the back of a pickup truck all the way from Monterey. As we drove in the open air along the curving coastline between mountains and ocean, I felt like I was in a postcard. I had never experienced scenery so beautiful in my entire life. That trip was over forty-three years ago and yet I can still recall the sensations I had while we travelled in the back of that bumpy truck: the smell of the salt air from the ocean below, the sight of waves crashing against rocks while the majestic stature of the mountains with towering redwood trees soared above. I didn't think about anything but the spectacular moment I was in. Gary jokingly threatened that if I said one more time how beautiful it was, he was going to throw me over the edge. We trekked into our campsite at Big Sur and stayed for one week. I wanted to stay forever.

A trip to the hospital brought me back to reality. Of course, Gary had to have a souvenir from every hospital along the way. In the middle of the night he had pain in his chest and thought he was having a heart attack. With the help of people camping near us, park rangers located our campsite and arranged an ambulance to take us to the Community Hospital of the Monterey Peninsula. After several tests with no indication that anything was wrong, we came to learn that Gary had had an anxiety attack. While I was living in a suspended state of bliss, Gary was dealing with anxiety. I didn't realize that he hadn't called his parents in over a month and they didn't even know he was in California.

Feeling upset and guilty, Gary decided it was time for him to leave. He still needed two grade thirteen credits in order to graduate from high school and thought it best that he enrol in school for September.

I didn't want to go home. Did I even have a home to go to? I wanted to keep travelling and came up with a plan to go to Mexico on my own. I wasn't ready to go back and face reality. We made our way to San Francisco, both hitchhiking and taking the bus as our means of transportation. We were at the airport and I was still trying to figure out what to do. I was scared to travel alone, but also frightened of the uncertainty I would have to deal with back home. I hadn't thought about Daddy's death or my future at all when I was away. Gary was against the idea of me travelling by myself and thought it wasn't safe.

He suggested I go back to Toronto and then plan a trip to Mexico from there. Maybe Tori or another friend could come with me. This made sense. I could go back, but just temporarily.

My stomach lurched as the plane took off, dreading the journey back to a home that no longer existed.

Chapter 62
Homeless

IT WAS SICKENING TO SEE MY FATHER'S POSSESSIONS LAID OUT ON the driveway displayed like cheap wares at a flea market. I was against having a garage sale to get rid of Daddy's things, but I had been away and wasn't the one who had to deal with the many details that come after death: selling the house, clearing out all the contents. I watched as neighbours haggled over the price of a pipe from my father's collection, books he had read, records he had played. I chose a few tokens of Daddy's life, including a painting and a ceramic sculpture. The painting by Austrian realist painter Otto Eichinger was of an old man holding a glass of red wine. Daddy loved the fine detail that showed each small wrinkle in the man's face. The ceramic sculpture, only ten inches tall, was also a depiction of an old man – an organ grinder sitting on a stump wearing tattered clothes, a top hat, and smoking a pipe. On top of his organ he is holding sheet music in his veined and wrinkled hand with the lyrics "O Sole Mio" written in tiny print. A dachshund also wearing a top hat is cuddled up against the man's leg. These two pieces of art reflected men content in their later years. They both displayed a carefree, untroubled expression; a life that was out of my father's grasp and an age he never reached.

I moved in with Connie, Saul, and the kids, sharing a bedroom with Jessica, who was a toddler. I nicknamed her "Jessica jujube" as I thought her skin went as red as a jujube when she cried; also she was so sweet. Jessica was innocent and joyful, the antithesis of all that I was feeling. I envied the bliss of her ignorance. I was at such a different stage of life than my sister Connie. I went out often to see Tori, Gary, and my friends. I didn't invite them over to Connie's house, since there wasn't room or privacy. I felt that my comings and goings in her home were an intrusion. She was busy with her demanding work and family life and I was adding to her responsibilities. I felt misplaced, in the way, and thought it best I stay somewhere else while working on my escape to Mexico. I called Wendy to see if I could come and live with her. She was leaving to travel for several months and said I could take her room on Brunswick Avenue, where she shared the top floor of a house with two other roommates: Ryan, a gay man who worked at Hassle Free Health Clinic, and Stefanie, a journalist. They were both much older than me and, while I had met them before, I didn't know them well. It was odd how Brunswick Avenue kept popping up in my life. It was where I had lived with Neil, and the Brunswick House was the tavern where my father had met the waitress he'd had an affair with. Neither of these were pleasant memories, and I didn't want to live downtown, but I had limited choices and it would only be temporary.

I asked Tori if she wanted to travel with me to Mexico, but she had already organized a trip to Greece. When she suggested I go with her, I readily abandoned my plans. She said she was thrilled to have me as a travel companion. I felt relief and comfort in knowing she wanted me with her. She was leaving in October and wanted to go for a significant length of time – four or five months – perfect for me – the longer the better.

Chapter 63
Greece

GARY TOOK US TO THE AIRPORT. IT WAS A TEARFUL GOODBYE. I HAD no home, job, or purpose, and Gary understood my need to leave. I was adrift, but the one thing I knew for sure was that travelling would bring adventure, freedom, and relief. I could be in a foreign country far away from the familiar landscape of grief. It was hard to leave Gary, but my absence would allow him to concentrate on completing his last two grade thirteen credits.

After the cost of airfare – seven hundred dollars – Tori and I budgeted five hundred dollars each for spending. Our goal was to make our money last as long as possible by living simply, staying in hostels and pensions (guest houses). However, we weren't going to penny-pinch to extend the trip or deny ourselves simple pleasures – like good food. When the money ran out, we would come home. We filled our backpacks with a change of clothes – three layers for warmth, a bathing suit, and a towel – and set off to explore.

It was 1976, a time when many young people put on a backpack and travelled the world. It was safe, affordable, and accessible. Our five hundred dollars each lasted for four months, from October to January.

After a nine-hour flight, it was a culture shock to arrive in Athens and not be able to speak the language or navigate the streets or bus system to find the hostel we were staying in. Everywhere we went men made clucking noises at us, stared at us, heckled us. We stood out – two young teenage girls travelling on their own. With our light-coloured hair – Tori's white-blond bob and my shoulder-length wavy golden locks – we beamed like a flashlight against the dark-haired Greeks. We ignored the unwanted attention of men. It was more annoying than frightening. If we ordered them to "go away" in an assertive voice, they seemed to listen like berated little schoolboys. Our rule was to always stay together. There were only a few close calls we had to deal with.

Once, we took a short side trip to Izmir, Turkey, for a weekend, and when I went to use the common bathroom in our hotel, a Turkish man came barging in trying to grab me. When Tori heard me scream, she ran down the hall and, with a courage and strength I'd never seen before, punched the guy in the face. While he registered the shock of being assaulted by a woman, we escaped.

Another time, on the tiny island of Antiparos, a uniformed police officer approached us as we sat by the water's edge. He said something in Greek that we couldn't understand. "Me-las an-glee-ka? Do you speak English?" we asked. We kept urging him to repeat his statement, explain what he was saying. Since he was a cop, we thought it was important to understand what he was trying to tell us. After at least ten reiterations, we realized he wasn't speaking Greek at all, but was repeating in English: "Would you like to suck my penis?"

"Óchi efcharistó" – No thank you, we said, like polite Canadian girls. Once we got away, we laughed at how we had kept asking him to repeat his disgusting request over and over. We learned it wasn't safe to trust the police in Greece.

We stayed in Athens just long enough to take in the history and beauty of the Acropolis, eat moussaka and Greek salad, and drink retsina at the Poseidon café, and then we mapped out our itinerary for the islands we wanted to visit: Lesvos, Samos, Paros, Ios, Santorini, and Crete.

Our goal was to be travellers, not tourists. We wanted to live with the locals, settling in one place long enough to get to know the community, eat regional food, and get a true sense of the place. We rented rooms from residents that were cheap – two dollars a night. In Ios, we rented a room that cost us only sixty dollars for the entire month. On each island we visited we stayed at least two weeks and sometimes up to a month, always creating a cozy abode in our rental unit. Most of the places we stayed didn't have a shower or had limited hot water. At one room we rented we had access to hot water once a week and we luxuriated in shampooing our hair outside on the open-air white-washed concrete courtyard that overlooked the turquoise Mediterranean. For those in-between bad hair days, Tori and I purchased Greek scarves with colourful byzantine shield motifs that we wore like babushkas.

We bought a small gas burner so we could cook a pot of food in our room if we didn't want to eat out at a restaurant. Cauliflower with cheese sauce and a salad of locally grown tomatoes, cucumbers, and olives was a favourite evening meal. In every village we stayed in, we would discover the best local bakery and begin our day with a walk to the pastry shop for a freshly baked, warm loaf of brown bread and a steaming-hot cup of Nescafé for breakfast. Lunches on the beach or in our room included sardines, crackers, feta cheese, and figs. When we wanted dinner out, we splurged and spent five dollars each for steak, french fries, and Greek salad at the taverna. We often lingered at the taverna until late in the evening, learning how to play backgammon with locals over many glasses of retsina and demestica wine or aperitifs of ouzo and banana liquor.

We befriended locals who shared with us their family-oriented, simpler way of life. In Lesvos, we met George and Manos, two young men fluent in English who were our age and best friends just like us. They were our local tour guides. Manos took us home for lunch, where his mother cooked us fresh fish. We hung out at a fort built in 5000 BC while George played his bouzouki and they both sang old Greek folk songs. The setting was magical, romantic, and timeless. It made me long for Gary. I wondered how I was going to be able to be apart from him for such an extended length of time. When we said goodbye to George and Manos after several weeks in Lesvoz, George slipped a note into my pocket, telling me to read it later.

Dear Marsha

This was the last time you saw me. I really loved you. Don't laugh. Yes, I did and I do. I'm just leaving, going to school. I've nothing else to tell you except that I loved you too much. Good by and thanks for everything. George

While it was charming, I had felt George looking at me with desire and I didn't feel ardour toward him at all. There was no way I was going to embark on any romantic adventures. My heart belonged to Gary.

In Ios, a tiny island with no cars and a mass of white-washed houses built against a cliff, we made friends with other travellers from around the world. We stayed for a month, developing relationships that created a close-knit family. We hung out with Gwen and Don, a couple travelling together from B.C. who were older than us, but age difference didn't matter; Gaston, who played the guitar, and Louis, who played the flute, were both from Quebec and provided us with musical serenades; Pascal from France – who only spoke French – had been travelling on his own but made fast friends with Gaston and Louis; Greg, from Australia, was travelling on his own as well and was glad to connect with our friendly group. Our room tended to be the gathering spot, with its wooden table, four chairs, and cozy floor rugs. We spent day and night conversing in both English and French. My high-school French, while limited, came in handy.

Late one night, Greg knocked on our door, looking for company. I learned that Greg, like me, had experienced the sudden death of his father.

Tori went to bed and I ended up talking to Greg all night about grief. He told me that high winds and poor architecture caused the arena – where his dad had been curling – to collapse, crushing his father to death. Greg also lost close friends in the terrible accident.

I was glad to be able to talk to someone about death and loss. I felt alone in my grief. It also put things in perspective. I thought I had the worst luck, but after talking to Greg I realized that there were others who were dealing with death and that it takes time to get over it. Greg's father had died three years before, but he said he'd woken up the other night crying because he'd dreamt his father was alive. I shared my own dreams – often nightmares – about Daddy and how I was fearful about my own mortality. One night, I woke up after a nightmare and was scared to go back to sleep. I couldn't feel my heart beating. I was weak and thought my life had come to an end. Ever since Daddy died, I had this irrational fear that I, too, was going to die. After talking to Greg, I could see that it was going to take me years to recover from the trauma of finding my father dead on the floor.

Tori and I were perfect travel companions. We were compatible in every way – drawn to the same places, people, and pace. We eased into a relaxing routine of reading, visiting with friends, planning and eating our daily meals, walking to the beach, and working on our needlepoints. Inspired by the beauty of the Greek landscape, we had purchased canvas and thread in a little village in Samos, creating our own colourful tapestries to work on throughout our trip. Tori was far more artistic than me, but I enjoyed the simple process of stitching the needle in and out of the tiny holes, marvelling as a depiction of the golden sun and turquoise sea emerged. At night we would go to the taverna for drinks – the retsina and ouzo always flowed freely – with our new friends. There was no television, no radio – the Internet wasn't yet invented – so sometimes in the evening, if we couldn't sleep or didn't want to go out, I would be the entertainment. Tori loved listening to stories and I liked telling them. I shared the entire plots of romantic sagas like *Wuthering Heights*, *Jayne Eyre*, and *Doctor Zhivago* over our four months together.

During my time in Greece I gained a sense of community, peace, contentment, and twenty pounds! With daily (sometimes twice a day) trips to the bakery for bread, cream pies, and kourabiethes – the delicious Greek shortbread almond cookies covered in confectioners sugar – as well as all the alcohol we consumed – the two pairs of pants that I brought were bulging at the seams.

I pined for Gary. From the journal that I kept every day of our trip:

> My whole being aches for Gary. I have decided that I will phone him. I worry a lot and hope he is alright. I'm going to make the phone call at 9:00 p.m. which will be 2:00 in the afternoon, his time. I'm nervous and excited. I hope he will be home.

To make a phone call on any of the islands, it had to be arranged a day in advance with an operator. The operator would then inform the intended recipient to let them know the expected day and time of the call. It wasn't entirely precise. Sometimes you would get to the phone booth and it would be occupied or the operator wouldn't be available.

The day that the operator put my call through, Gary's mother answered. She said that Gary had just left for an appointment and wasn't home. It felt strange to talk to her and I didn't really know what to say. After an uncomfortable silence, I said goodbye and hung up. I was devastated. I had anticipated being able to hear Gary's voice and know that he was okay. I also felt insecure. Why had he gone out when he knew I would be calling? Did he miss me, like I missed him? Did he still love me?

It was hard to shake my worry and anxiety, especially being so far away. I tried to stay positive and think there must be an explanation. When a letter from Gary arrived ten days later at the post office, my trembling fingers could hardly open it.

> Dear Marsha
>
> I feel like shit. I'm sorry I missed your phone call. The operator said you would phone at 2:00 p.m. the next day. I waited from 12:30- 2:45 and then went out for a minute. I rushed

back home and you had phoned. I just couldn't believe it. I am sitting here in fucking tears, hoping you didn't think I would miss your call on purpose. I have been waiting to talk to you. God-damn-it! Don't you realize how much I miss you? I am thinking of you day in and day out. I need you and miss you. I love you so much sometimes I feel like I can't communicate to anyone but you. I need you now more than ever. I can only hope you are safe and happy.

Please take care

Gary

I was delirious. I felt like the heroine in the films I had been recounting to Tori. Gary was my Heathcliff, my Mr. Rochester, my Yuri Zhivago.

I was ready to go home.

Chapter 64
Home

BEING IN GREECE PROVIDED ME WITH TIME FOR REFLECTION AND perspective. I not only thought about Daddy's death, but I considered his life, my life, and our life together. I regretted how I had treated him: what I'd put him through with my wild parties, moving out with Neil, our estrangement for two years. I wished that I had treated him differently. He'd been difficult to live with, but so had I. I lamented that I was not emotionally close with him. He was my father, the only parent I had in my world, so I felt affection for him, but I couldn't say I loved him. I felt sorry for him. His life was short and lonely.

I was grateful that I moved back home with him when I did and that we had time to restore our relationship. Those nine months gave birth to something new and different for me. My view of my father had altered. I came to appreciate and accept him, recognizing that he wasn't going to change. I forgave him for being imperfect, for being an asshole. He was doing the best he could with the cards he'd been dealt. All he really wanted was love and connection, which, in hindsight, I can see eluded him.

I thought back to our dinners at The Steak Pit, his pessimistic view of life as being filled with cloudy days. Certainly, in my nineteen years he had weathered many storms: the death of my mother, Carol's suicide, his divorce from Brenda, the abandonment of an illegitimate son. Who could he turn to for advice, comfort? He, too, had lost his parents to death. What must it have been like for a man to raise three daughters on his own at a time when the role of men was to be a provider, not a nurturer? There were no role models for him. Who knew what demons he carried around from the hurt and pain he had suffered in his life? I don't think it was a coincidence that he dropped dead of a heart attack. His heart simply couldn't take it anymore.

I believe I brought some joy into my father's life during our last months together. We shared meals, we laughed, told stories about daily events, and we didn't fight. We got along. In hindsight, these ordinary moments – which at the time seemed inconsequential –bring comfort to me now. I've learned that it's not the splashy events in life – that we pour time and money into – that matter, but it's the rituals and routines of our everyday existence that hold significance. To be able to be present in the moment, connect with others, and show loving kindness is the way to live life. My experience of loss and grief has sharpened my senses to the sweetness and preciousness of life. I try not to take anything for granted and am grateful every morning I wake up alive, healthy, and able to feel love. We are all only one breath away from death, so I want to use my time wisely.

Daddy told me he loved me. I don't feel guilt that I couldn't reciprocate those words. I cared about him in a real and genuine way. That was enough.

As our flight from Greece began its descent into Toronto, I thought about home. What was I going home to? What was home? Was it a place? I no longer had a physical home – 77 Plymbridge had been sold to a new family that would make it theirs. The place I was born and raised in no longer existed for me. In my time away with Tori, I had felt a sense of belonging, connection, and community with her, the people we met, and the experiences we shared. I felt safe. Perhaps home wasn't tied to place at all, but was a feeling – of love, trust, mutual caring. I felt this with Gary.

I had imagined the moment of my reunion with Gary at the airport. He'd written to say he would pick Tori and me up. I hoped I hadn't romanticized it into some schmaltzy Hollywood scene. I was nervous; feeling excitement, anticipation, and a tiny bit of fear. What if he wasn't there? What if I didn't feel love? What if he didn't?

Tori and I were in the baggage-claim area waiting for our backpacks when I saw him. How like Gary to make his way into a restricted area. We ran to each other and kept embracing and pulling away to look at each other, trying to register that this was reality. He had his coat off and he kept whipping it up and down on the floor like he was beating a rug, saying over and over, "I can't believe you're here!"

"I'm here. I'm home."

Epilogue

RELIVING THE STORY OF MY YOUTH AND PUTTING WORDS INTO print has evoked joy, pain, sorrow, and liberation. I feel fortunate that I had the time and privilege to write and gain perspective on some of the pleasures and challenges in my youth. In the ensuing forty-four years I have lived another life. Since there will not likely (never say never) be a book about the subsequent years, I feel an obligation to satisfy the reader's curiosity, to know what happened next.

Gary and I were married on a gorgeous hot sunny day on July 14, 1979, in the large backyard of Connie and Saul's newly purchased home. I was twenty-two years old and Gary was twenty-one. We had our reception on Captain John's Harbour Boat Restaurant, a former Adriatic passenger ship that was docked at the foot of Yonge Street on Queens Quay West. We were the first of our friends to get married and it was a wild night of partying – the cops were called due to the illegal smoking of pot on the upper deck of the ship. On the lower deck, Wendy lit up a lawful cigar that Daddy had put away, saving it, he said, for my wedding day. The photographs capture us as a young couple full of love and hope for the future.

It didn't end happily ever after.

Our marriage met the same fate as the doomed ship where we had our wedding reception. Captain John's fell into disrepair, bankruptcy, and ultimately had to be towed away for scrap. When people asked us, "How long have you been married?" Gary always responded in the same way: "Ten happy years – but together for nineteen." We definitely had some good years and our union produced two wonderful, well-adjusted, successful children – Sarah born in 1987 and Garrett born in 1991 – whom we raised together.

I know now that the early loss of my mother – as well as the many other losses in my life – resulted in a fear of abandonment that I carried into my intimate relationship with Gary. Coupled with my worldview of needing to be self-reliant, these two unconscious processes worked in tandem to create a self-fulfilling prophecy of not allowing myself to count on, or depend on, anyone.

Gary had his own issues to deal with, but that is his story to tell.

After an acrimonious divorce, we have now come full circle, sharing many joyous occasions together: the weddings of Sarah and Garrett and our new role as grandparents. I believe my memoir is a testament to the love and devotion Gary and I once shared. I was inspired to tell my story by, and for, both of my children. My early life shaped who I am as a woman and a mother. I hope the insight gained about my past informs their present as they begin their own journey of becoming parents.

Gary remarried and found the love, peace, and contentment he deserves.

I also remarried, and have found in Elwood an unconditional love, acceptance, and belonging that I never knew existed. With him my worldview has shifted. I know that I can count on him to always be there for me, as I am for him. I am also fortunate to have two bonus daughters, Sam, and Robin, who have enriched and enhanced my life.

While both my sisters now live in Vancouver, they continue to be a significant presence in my life and I feel fortunate to call them both family and friends. This memoir is personal to me – my perspective and my memories may not be theirs. I hope my account evokes laughter, understanding, and forgiveness – for me, themselves, and our father.

My friend Tori continues to play a pivotal role in my life and we are still bosom buddies. There are other female friends who are unnamed in this book – they know who they are – and whom I consider family. They are not my biological sisters, but the ones I have chosen to go through life with. All of them were there for many of the events that I describe in these pages. I could not have survived without them. They are unnamed simply due to decisions made to move the narrative in my story forward and focus on key themes.

There is one group of women – we call ourselves "the girls" – who went to elementary and junior high school together and we have been going to our annual "girls weekend" at a cottage for the past forty-six years. We also take trips together and have shared the highs and lows of our life over the decades. While they were there during my early years and know me well, I hope my account provides even more insight into my past, identifying the significant role they played and continue to play in my life.

I spent a career in Early Childhood Education, working with children, families, and communities and ultimately as a professor at Humber College, trying to impart knowledge about the significant role that adults play in creating a sense of belonging for all children. I hope my own story inspires others to reflect on the power they have to make a difference in the life of a child.

It has always been my strong belief (and there is now research to support this) that attachment in the early years plays a pivotal role in shaping a child's future. While I lost my mother at an early age, I am thankful that I received her unconditional love. However brief my relationship with her was, it was a gift that continues across generations.

The definition of orphan varies, but it's commonly understood as a child who has lost both parents either through death, disappearance, abandonment, separation, or loss. At age nineteen, I earned the distinction of being labelled an orphan. To declare yourself an orphan often evokes sympathy or pity from others, and while I felt shame and an otherness growing up, I can now appreciate my ability to weather the many storms of my youth. My father, Gil as his friends called him, always thought life had more cloudy days than sunny ones, but my belief is that the joy of life is felt more keenly when one has experienced pain or loss. Today I feel true happiness *because* I have known sadness. I experience love *because* I have had loss. I appreciate sunny days much more profoundly *because* of the clouds.

There's a fine line between disaster and survival, but this orphan is grateful to have weathered the storm and landed safely ashore.

Acknowledgements

Thank-you to:

Humber College School for Writers where I had the privilege and humbling experience of being a student after twelve years of sitting on the other side of the desk.

Diane Schoemperlen, my mentor, for her guidance, inspiration, and thorough, timely, thoughtful review. Your belief in me as a writer propelled me forward.

Heather Sangster of Strong Finish Editorial Design for her impeccable attention to detail.

Gary O'Neill for his feedback and encouragement.

Trish Bain for her kinship, fervour, and painstaking reading of my manuscript.

Suzan Wookey, Kim Chapple, and Alison Bates for lifelong friendship, support, and sisterhood.

My birth sisters who figure so prominently in my past, present and future. You both model leadership, positivity, and chutzpah.

Ranya Khan, Tara Lew, Carol Appleby, and Nazlin Hirji — extraordinary educators, friends, book lovers, and constant cheerleaders.

Hilary O'Neill, Jay Springthorpe, and Wendy Barrett for continually asking me to read my "stories" aloud and always responding with laughter and tears.

Sarah O'Neill Springthorpe and Garrett O'Neill, whose enthusiasm inspired, motivated, and encouraged me. From conception to completion you were my unceasing champions. Without the contribution of your exceptional skills — everything from photography to web site design to marketing — I could not have accomplished all of this without you.

Finally, to my love and life partner, Elwood Shantz, who listened, read, edited, praised, reviewed, and cared about every single sentence. He was with me every step of this emotional journey. Wherever you are is home.